THE STORY OF HILLEBRAND ESTATES WINERY

The Story of Hillebrand Estates Winery

Peter G. Mielzynski-Zychlinski

KEY PORTER BOOKS

Canadian Cataloguing in Publication Data

Mielzynski-Zychlinski, Peter G. (Peter Gerhard), 1922–
    The story of Hillebrand Estates Winery

Includes index.
ISBN 1-55263-315-2

1. Hillebrand Estates Winery. 2. Wine and wine making – Ontario – Niagara-on-the-Lake Region – History. I. Title.

HD 9384.C34H54 2001   338.7'6632'00971338   C00-933140-9

THE CANADA COUNCIL | LE CONSEIL DES ARTS
FOR THE ARTS | DU CANADA
SINCE 1957 | DEPUIS 1957

The publisher gratefully acknowledges the support of the Canada Council for the Arts and the Ontario Arts Council for its publishing program.

We acknowledge the financial support of the Government of Canada through the Book Publishing Industry Development Program (BPIDP) for our publishing activities.

Key Porter Books Limited
70 The Esplanade
Toronto, Ontario
Canada M5E 1R2

www.keyporter.com

Electronic formatting: Heidi Palfrey
Design: Patricia Cavazzini
Map drawn by John Lightfoot

Printed and bound in Canada

01 02 03 04 05 06 6 5 4 3 2 1

CONTENTS

FOREWORD

The Ontario wine industry has confounded the naysayers. Today everyone wants to jump on its bandwagon. New wineries spring up every week, and prices for vineyard land in the province have skyrocketed. Even the French want to buy into the dream (Vincor has a joint venture with the Burgundian shippers Boisset for a new winery in Niagara-on-the-Lake as well as a vineyard project with La Groupe Tailian, a Bordeaux company, in British Columbia's Okanagan Valley). And Ontario Icewine, that reward of winter, has become an international cult wine.

But a mere 19 years ago when Peter Mielzynski negotiated the purchase of Newark Wines on behalf of a Swiss-based company and his own importing agency, the future for Canadian wines looked bleak indeed. In order to sell their wines in those years Canadian companies had to "disguise" them as French and German products, even co-opting the names of European regions to do so.

The pioneers who turned the industry around—Donald Ziraldo and Karl Kaiser at Inniskillin, Paul Bosc at Château des Charmes and Peter Gamble as executive director of the fledgling Vintners Quality Alliance—have been rightfully honored. But Peter Mielzynski, laboring in the background, saw the commercial possibilities of an industry then in its doldrums long before the others.

A born salesman, Peter is happiest when he is walking around wine stores, speaking to potential customers. But there is nothing slick or superficial about his salesmanship because Peter is a gentleman of the old school who delights in personal communication and gentle persuasion. In this book he gives credit to everyone else for the success of Hillebrand Estates, but it was his vision and his energy that created the climate for this to happen. The Ontario wine industry owes him a great debt of gratitude.

—Tony Aspler

1

STEPPING BACK
IN TIME

*I*n 1949 I immigrated to Canada full of youthful enthusiasm and eyes wide open to a land of opportunity. It wasn't long before I discovered my true passion—sales and marketing. Fortunately, Larry McGuinness, owner of McGuinness Distillery, realized my abilities, and through him I landed in the fledgling Canadian wine-and-spirits industry where, over the years, I have been able to play a role in its development. It has been a time characterized by enormous change, and I had the unique opportunity to experience those changes firsthand and in some instances to influence some of them.

In 1958 I started out with McGuinness Distillery, a company that both manufactured and imported spirits and liqueurs. It was an exciting time with broad horizons and brilliant opportunities for the entrepreneurial spirit. And it held my interest for 21 years.

In 1979 I launched my own company, Peter Mielzynski Agencies Ltd., representing wines and spirits that were sold through the provincial liquor boards across the country. In 1982 I spearheaded the purchase of a small Niagara winery on behalf of our company and an outside partner, and proceeded to build, in just a few years, what would be considered one of Canada's premier wineries, with products ready to compete on the world wine stage.

This is the part of my journey I will share with you in this book: the explosive growth of the Canadian wine industry, as seen through the window of our winery.

But first some history.

Back in 1958, when I was traveling from province to province with the McGuinness Distillery, I found that only Quebec customers could find a decent choice of imported wines in their liquor stores. French Canadians have always been fond of wines—ever since the first French explorers arrived in the New World. In Ontario the first license was not issued until 1937, so the variety of wines in the province's hotels and restaurants was not as great as in Quebec. In Canada's capital, Ottawa, temporary home to many international visitors, people who wanted a glass of wine with a restaurant meal often traveled across the river to Hull, in Quebec, in order to enjoy a wider selection. Not surprisingly, in the eyes of the rest of the country, La Société des Alcools du Québec (S.A.Q.) was considered to be the connoisseur of imported wines and spirits. When discussing new wine listings with other provincial liquor boards, the buyer's first question always was: "How is the wine selling in Quebec?"

When I started with McGuinness Distillery in the late 1950s, we were just at the point of introducing Sichel's Blue Nun Liebfraumilch (750-mL [25-oz.] bottle for $2.75 and a 350-mL [12-oz.] bottle for $1.55—those were the days!) to the Ontario market. German wines were being introduced to Canada, mainly by Canadian soldiers who had served with the Allied Forces in West Germany. Blue Nun was an easy name to remember and the wine was medium dry, making it suitable with any food. It could also be enjoyed as a cocktail. Blue Nun became a very popular wine. Following its success, many other German wines started to appear at liquor control board stores across Canada.

At the same time there was massive Italian immigration to Canada. Most of the new immigrants came from Calabria and Sicily, where drinking wine was an integral part of daily life. Making wine to drink at home was also part of the culture they brought with them to Canada. As a result, these new Canadians seldom purchased wine from liquor stores. Indeed, the Liquor Control Board of Ontario helped Italian immigrants by allowing them to import grapes from California, strictly for making homemade wines.

I remember that every September and October many Italian Canadians, who wanted to buy used whiskey and brandy barrels for their homemade wines, visited McGuinness Distillery. We used to charge them $3 a barrel. We never had enough used barrels to satisfy the demand! We also supplied them with McGuinness Anisette, Crème de Menthe and, their favorite, Coffee Liqueur, to celebrate family weddings and christenings. But homemade red wine continued to be their beverage of choice for day-to-day consumption.

When the new immigrants from Italy arrived in North America in the fifties, their expansive hospitality soon influenced popular culture. In no time traditional pasta dishes became widely accepted. Gradually Canadians were being introduced to European cuisine and wines. They began to change their eating habits. The liquor control boards responded to these demands by carrying an increasing variety of table wines. Italian wines, in particular, offered the variety people sought at a reasonable price.

In 1968 I paid a visit to Tommy Richards, who was at that time the purchasing director of the Alberta Liquor Control Board in Edmonton. A well-known and respected connoisseur of wines and spirits, he mentioned during our meeting that the Alberta Liquor Control Board was looking to sell Italian red and white table wines in 2-liter-size (68-oz.) bottles. He did not have to repeat himself. I was sure that he had also told our competitors what he was looking for. I wanted to be the first to present the board with an application and suitable samples of Italian wines.

That evening I took a flight via London to Milan. I met with the managing director of the Gruppo Italiano Vini, Dr. Alberto de Marchi, whose wines were already represented elsewhere in Canada by

McGuinness Distillery. We drove to their Lamberti Winery, situated near Verona, to meet Mr. E. Pedron, director of Lamberti and chief winemaker for Gruppo Italiano Vini. He helped me to compare all the available labels and bottles, and organized wine tastings so that I could select the right wines.

I was back in Tommy Richards's Edmonton office the following week, with samples of red and white Donini, Vino de Verona. In a short time this pair became the best-selling wines in Alberta. Within one year they were listed in every province across Canada. As their popularity grew, they realized sales of more than 700,000 cases a year. Besides the Donini wines there were many other Italian wines listed at this time, including Colli Albani, which became very successful in Ontario.

French wines were not far behind. At this time the Kressmann Company introduced Kressmann Selectionné table wines to the Canadian market. They became the most popular table wines sold in Canada. Just a few years before, wine had been consumed regularly only in Quebec. Now there was a marked change. Consumers across the country wanted a broader selection of wines from which to choose. The baby boomers were coming of age. Many had been exposed to cultures with rich traditions in food and wine. In this context, the government-run monopolies, which controlled alcohol distribution, seemed antiquated. No one could have expected that, within a few years, Canada would become such a flourishing wine market. It was the advent of self-service stores that changed wine consumption habits so dramatically. Now consumers had real choice.

In 1967 the first self-service liquor store in Canada opened in Regina, Saskatchewan. The new system, where customers could actually see all the available brands and could make a purchase without going through a set of complicated procedures, was a welcome change. Initially, some customers felt a little overwhelmed by the choice, but they soon adapted. It is important to remember that in the 1950s customers needed an order form to buy wines and spirits, and that into the 1960s, consumers could not see or touch a bottle of wine or spirits without first filling out a form! All of a sudden there was no bureaucracy (with its attendant moral overtones) to separate the buyer from the product. After a while, customers became comfortable with self-service stores and found it interesting to browse, read the labels and discover wines and spirits from many countries of the world.

The second self-service liquor store opened in Vancouver in the Park Royal area in September 1969. The grand opening of this store took place just before the Annual Convention of the Liquor Control Boards and the Association of the Canadian Distillers at the Muskoka Sands resort in Ontario. I was in Vancouver on business at the time. I was so impressed that I could not resist filming the new store, so that I could show it to delegates at our upcoming convention. It was the first day, and customers were still slightly uneasy shopping in a self-service liquor store. While I was filming, one customer got so upset with me that she wanted me to destroy the film. She was afraid that I was taking pictures for a magazine and that she would be recognized by her friends. Prohibition had been over for 50 years, but the link between alcohol and guilt was as evident as ever!

It took liquor control boards in the West some time to convert their conventional stores to self-service stores. One reason for the delay was that their staff was not suitably prepared. With the coming of self-service stores, it was essential to have a well-informed staff who could answer customers' questions about their many products. The Alberta Liquor Control Board was the fastest to convert their stores to self-service, as Tommy Richards was able to help in their education program. The British Columbia, Saskatchewan and Manitoba boards were very thankful when I made a proposal to arrange for Gerry Ayling, the McGuinness agency manager, who was extremely knowledgeable and experienced, to travel from province to province giving wine and spirit lectures to groups of store managers.

Before the introduction of self-service stores there was no in-centive for customers to experiment with something new. These "conventional stores," as they were later called, reinforced the status quo. Ontario had the most complicated system. In conventional stores all the brands available in that particular store were listed by category on the board. The customer had to complete a purchase slip, giving the name of the brand, the price and the number. The slip had to be signed by the customer and taken to the cashier for payment. Since the bottles were not on display, but stored in bins, the serving clerk would hand a bottle, discreetly wrapped in a brown paper bag, to the customer, and, according to provincial law, the customer had to take the bottle straight home.

Despite a slow start, the western provinces were way ahead of conservative Ontario. It was only in 1969 that the first self-service store was opened in the province, in Weston. Many other stores soon followed. Finally, the Liquor Control Board of Ontario (LCBO) decided to make shopping for wine and liquor more enjoyable. There was no doubt that the introduction of self-service stores changed shopping habits. The new system brought legitimacy and education to the liquor industry. There was nothing to hide.

When customers suddenly had access to a large variety of imported table wines, Ontario wines, which at the time were made largely from Labrusca grapes (North American indigenous grape variety), did not do well. The Canadian wine industry, made up mainly of large wineries, did not believe that the Ontario wine regions could successfully produce hybrids and vinifera grapes (European vine stocks). While suitable for blending to make nonalcoholic grape juice, Labrusca grapes, when used for table wine, impart an unpleasant character. It is ironic that Brights Winery owned a viticulture research station located on Highway 55, and in 1955 produced the first Canadian Chardonnay from vines imported from France! Unfortunately, this experiment didn't last.

The Ontario government found itself in a dilemma. In order to improve the quality of their products, wineries wanted to be allowed to import bulk wines for blending. On the other hand, the Ontario government had tried, without success, to encourage grape growers to grow more European-type hybrid vine, which could eventually replace the Labrusca grapes. Sadly, Ontario grape growers did not want to invest in this project. Labrusca grapes had high yields and were the easiest to produce. A further disincentive to change was that the Ontario government bought any Labrusca grapes the growers could not sell. The majority of the Labrusca growers in the Niagara Peninsula believed that the government would protect them, for political reasons, to the bitter end.

In 1976, the Ontario government allowed wineries to import bulk wines or grape juice to an overall volume of 15 percent but limited them to using no more than 30 percent in any one blend. This did not satisfy the large wineries. Their plans were to continue as bulk importers, blenders and bottlers. The message that was implicit in the Ontario government's ill-considered decision was that they did not believe that the Niagara Peninsula had the potential to become a world-class grape-growing area. And that did not go down well with the pioneers who were trying to produce high-quality wines. The government did not realize that the large wineries of Ontario would never achieve success unless the area earned the status as an acknowledged classical grape-growing region.

Meanwhile, the availability of an increasing variety of wines, imported from celebrated regions of the world, made the Canadian public eager to learn more about wines. Articles about wines and winemaking became more commonplace, and wine guides and encyclopedias were readily available in bookstores. Canadians discovered that every wine-producing country has a set of regulations that determine the standards for its finest products. They started to read the labels and learned the differences between "table wine," "table wine from a designated region" and "top-quality wine from a designated region."

In the 1970s the Niagara Peninsula did not have any recognized regulations that could set standards for quality wines. When regulations were set, in 1988, it was one of the defining moments for quality winemaking in Niagara.

There were, however, some enlightened grape growers in the Niagara region who in the mid-1970s did not see much future in continuing to grow the North American varieties, and they started to replace them with the classical varieties. The procedure required a great financial investment and very hard work. Each parcel of land had to be leveled and systematically drained to ensure proper water runoff. Only then could varieties be selected and the vines planted.

As in other enterprises, the making of high-quality wines required skill and a certain vision. At this juncture in Niagara there were a number of key players. In 1975 two entrepreneurs, Donald Ziraldo and his partner, Karl Kaiser, started the Inniskillin Winery, determined to produce only quality wines. They had the vision to plant vinifera vines, purchased from France and Germany, to enable production of European-style wines in Canada. Their pioneer work was an incentive for others to follow.

Paul Bosc, another pioneer of vinifera varieties, strongly believed in the future of the Niagara Peninsula. In 1978 he opened Château des Charmes Winery with his friend, lawyer Rodger Gordon, and produced an excellent quality Riesling and Chardonnay from grapes grown in his own vineyards.

Roman Prydatkewycz was the first grower in the Niagara area to plant commercial quantities of the red vinifera variety Merlot. He had developed a special canopy management technique in his vineyard to improve the ripeness and quality of his crop.

Ambitious growers like Peter Buis Sr. and his sons, Peter Jr. and Kevin, of Glenlake Vineyards, became very successful by growing world-class grapes as early as 1980.

Albrecht Seeger, who emigrated from Germany with his parents to Canada in 1978, purchased 26 hectares (65 acres) of land along the Niagara River and became, in a short time, one of the most successful pioneers in cultivating world-class grapes. By 1984, Albrecht's well-maintained vineyards expanded to 55 hectares (137 acres).

Ewald Reif immigrated to Canada from Germany and purchased a vineyard along the Niagara River in 1977. He invested a sizable amount of money to prepare his land, replacing the Labrusca vines with the Chardonnay, Gewürztraminer and Riesling vines. Through hard work and his knowledge of the art of viticulture, he became a pioneer grower of world-class grapes. Five years later he started Reif Estate Winery with his Geisenheim-educated nephew, Klaus Reif.

Joe Pohorly, a structural engineer and owner of Newark Winery, was, as early as 1965, growing French hybrids and vinifera grapes. A very talented painter and an accomplished winemaker, his artistry was evident not only in his paintings but also in his winemaking.

These were the true pioneers. Before we begin the Hillebrand story, I would like to pay tribute to those who helped pave the way for the Niagara Peninsula's transformation into a respected, world-class wine-growing region.

THE BIRTH
OF AN IDEA

aus Balken became the home of the Underberg family in 1872, when Hubert Underberg, the successful owner of H. Underberg-Albrecht Distillery in Rhineberg, Germany, purchased it. The impressive residence, built in 1600 and set in a large, well-kept park located near Xanten, northwest of Düsseldorf, was totally restored and modernized by Hubert Underberg. Great care was taken to maintain the original style and character of the property. To this day, many rooms are furnished with the original Biedermeier furniture. And, to this day, it belongs to the Underberg family.

I will never forget my first visit to Haus Balken in 1981. I was invited to participate in a pheasant shoot with the current owner, Hubert's grandson Emil Underberg, and his friends. I arrived just before dinner and was introduced to his wife, Tina, and his children, who were gathered together in their beautiful living room. In a very short time the Underberg family made me feel completely at home. It was the first of many visits, which combined business with pleasure, and I became very fond of all the family. Indeed, in his teens, my son Robert spent three and a half years living with the Underberg family.

Emil and Tina Underberg have three daughters and a son, Emil Jr., who was close to Robert in age. Two of Tina's nieces were also living at Haus Balken, being raised together with their cousins. The house was always open to friends and business associates from all corners of the globe.

It was in this gracious, old European estate that the Hillebrand story began in October 1981. I was enjoying a visit with the Underbergs, and Emil and I were talking about our favorite subject—the wine and liquor industry. Emil was very happy with the progress of Peter Mielzynski Agencies Ltd., the import company I had founded two years before with George Lubienski, and of which Emil was the largest shareholder. The company's portfolio of internationally known brands kept growing. Donini, Vino de Verona, had become the largest-selling Italian table and house wine in Canada. In 1980 we were selling 475,000 cases a year.

Emil and I discussed other investment opportunities in Canada. He, like many other businessmen in West Germany, did not like the proximity of the powerful Soviet army in communist-controlled East Germany. For that reason he was looking for safe investments in Canada. The Underberg family had been successful in the spirits-producing business for many generations, and he wanted to continue that tradition both at home and in Canada. Emil was interested in acquiring a winery in the Niagara region that would be represented by the Peter Mielzynski Agencies' sales forces, but he insisted that it was quality wines, not quantity, that he was interested in.

We were well aware of the challenges. As mentioned earlier, until roughly the mid-1970s, the conventional wisdom was that only North American grapes, such as Labrusca, could be grown success-fully in the Niagara region. This approach resulted in the high-volume production of inferior wines, which could not compete with the increasing variety of imports from well-established, mainly European, wine-producing countries. Aggressive entrepreneurial winemakers, such as Karl Kaiser of Inniskillin and Paul Bosc of

Château des Charmes, began experimenting by growing vinifera grapes from vines imported from Europe. Quality varietal wines, such as Chardonnay and Riesling, had begun to appear on the market, produced by Ontario wineries. But the region was still a long way off from being recognized across Canada, never mind internationally.

Emil and I discussed who else we would approach to lend their expertise to this project. Emil Underberg's Schlumberger Winery in Vienna, Austria, was a success story, producing the very popular *méthode champenoise* sparkling wine Schlumberger, Sekt. (The *méthode champenoise*, involving bottle fermentation, was pioneered in Champagne, France. Many New World winemaking regions, such as California, Australia and Canada, began using the *méthode champenoise* to make their classic sparkling wines.) The head of wine production and chief winemaker at Schlumberger Winery was Heinz Turk. He was the perfect "old world" wine consultant for this new venture. Another wine expert, Bernhard Breuer, president of Scholl and Hillebrand Winery in Rudesheim, another of Underberg's companies, also seemed like someone whose advice we should seek. Peter Mielzynski Agencies represented his brands, and we had built a solid working relationship. Bernhard was a very cosmopolitan and open-minded connoisseur. He knew the Niagara region well and was particularly impressed with the quality of wines produced in the Niagara-on-the-Lake area.

Emil and I agreed that on my return to Canada I would start investigating various options. First, there was the possibility of buying a well-established winery with its own stores in Ontario. The second option was to purchase 4 to 6 hectares (10 to 15 acres) along The Parkway or Highway 55, close to Niagara-on-the-Lake, and build a modern winery from scratch. The third alternative was to look for a small winery with potential for development.

I was already well acquainted with domestic wines. During our time with McGuinness Distillery, George Lubienski (who became president of Peter Mielzynski Agencies in 1979) and I had acquired considerable experience marketing the Calona Winery products from Kelowna, British Columbia. The Niagara region was very well known to me, as every year it had provided McGuinness with fresh fruits for their liqueurs.

In the early months of 1982 I took the first steps toward the winery project. From the wineries of the Niagara region I collected samples of Chardonnay, Gewürztraminer, Riesling, Vidal, Baco Noir, Maréchal Foch and several bottles of blended table wines. They were then sent to the Schlumberger Winery in Vienna for Heinz Turk and his team to taste and provide a quality assessment. I enclosed a map of the Niagara Peninsula wine regions and marked the areas that would be most suitable for building or buying a winery.

In March 1982 Bernhard Breuer visited Peter Mielzynski Agencies, and we discussed the concept of building or buying a winery. He was very interested in consulting on the project and extended his stay in Toronto to accompany me to Niagara to visit Inniskillin, Brights and Andrés wineries. We tasted the same wine samples as I had sent to Heinz Turk. This meant that when Heinz Turk's assessment arrived we would be able to compare it with ours. Bernhard and I agreed that most of the samples of Chardonnay and Riesling were fresh and fruity and surprisingly pleasant to drink. Maréchal Foch was red purple with a fruity aroma and Labrusca character. We felt this wine could improve with more ageing. Overall, Bernhard was sure that all the wines we tasted could be much improved by applying new techniques and modern equipment. Bernhard returned to Germany full of enthusiasm for the new venture.

As part of my market research I visited many domestic wine stores, to get a better idea of how products were being packaged and displayed. I was surprised to discover how little store clerks knew about their wines, or how or where they were produced. I decided that when we opened our own stores, staff training would be a primary concern. I believe knowledgeable staff add to the wine-buying experience.

Meanwhile, during sales meetings at Peter Mielzynski Agencies, representatives showed genuine interest in the prospect of adding good-quality Ontario wines to our portfolio. A growing number of hotels and restaurants were interested in including Ontario wines on their wine lists, due in large part to the very good publicity received by Inniskillin Winery. Donald Ziraldo, president of Inniskillin, was an exemplary promoter of his winery and the whole Niagara-on-the-Lake area, and had done an incredible job for the Canadian wine industry.

Everything pointed to this being an opportune time for Emil Underberg to invest in quality wine production in the Niagara region. I hired a respected colleague in the industry, George Sorensen, explained what we were looking for and asked him to look for options. Our search focused on the Niagara-on-the-Lake area.

Emil Underberg, accompanied by his group of advisers, arrived in Toronto on July 25, 1982. We had arranged visits to existing wineries and to potential sites on which we could build a modern winery. We began our explorations early in the morning of July 26 with a visit to Château Gai Winery in Niagara Falls. Its owners, Labatts Brewery, had decided to sell. It was a large, national winery with many of its own stores located throughout Ontario. Château Gai was producing mainly inexpensive, bulk table wines, in addition to sherries and ports. After meeting with the management of Labatts Brewery and discussing the conditions of sale, we promised to come back to them in a couple of days. There was plenty more to see.

Our next appointment was with Paul Bosc Sr., the major shareholder of the Château des Charmes Estates Winery in St. Davids. He had invited us for a tour of the winery and the vineyards. Paul Bosc was recognized as an experienced grape grower and an accomplished winemaker. Château des Charmes's varietal wines were already known to consumers and listed in many hotels and restaurants. The winery was simply equipped, but we were very impressed by the vineyards. The whole establishment was more or less what we were looking for, and there was great growth potential. Unfortunately, Bosc was not keen to sell. Furthermore, if he did decide to sell he wasn't sure if he would stay involved, and that is what we wanted—to build with his expertise and cooperation.

As it was getting very late, we went back to Toronto and had dinner at Emil's favorite restaurant, Hy's Steak House. Over a satisfying meal, we relaxed and discussed our plans. The main challenge, we acknowledged, was to develop quality Ontario wines that would rival the quality European imports appearing on the shelves of the liquor boards. Whether we built or bought a winery we would need to invest in state-of-the-art winemaking equipment and in a short time produce improved-quality local wines from the already available Niagara grapes. In order to specialize in vinifera varieties and *méthode champenoise* sparkling wines, we would have to develop a close, mutually beneficial partnership with the Niagara grape growers, primarily those from the Niagara-on-the-Lake area. There was much to consider.

We shared our favorable impressions of Château des Charmes and Paul Bosc, and wondered what tomorrow would bring.

The next day we had an early appointment with the owners of Newark Estates Winery, Joseph and Betty Pohorly. The winery was located on Highway 55 in the village of Virgil, just 6 kilometers (4 miles) from Niagara-on-the-Lake. I was looking forward to meeting Joseph Pohorly, who was well known in the Niagara area as a respected entrepreneur, an accomplished grape grower and a successful winemaker.

Joseph, or Joe, as he was called, was born, appropriately, in Vineland in 1932. His parents' house was surrounded by grape-growing farms. At an early age he became very interested in viticulture and the art of winemaking, to the extent that, as a young man, he became a keen amateur winemaker. After graduating from high school, Joe attended the University of Toronto, where he acquired both a Bachelor of Science and Bachelor of Education degree. Later he studied at the State University of New York in Buffalo, where he earned the professional appellations P.Engineering and P.Agriculture. After finishing his studies Joe became a technical consultant to the Lincoln County Board of Education. Because he was free during the summers, he had time to pursue his interests in viticulture (a complex science of growing the right grape vines suitable to soil and local climate conditions) and viniculture (the knowledge and process of producing wine).

In 1962, Joe purchased 4 hectares (10 acres) of peach orchard, and after clearing the land, he planted vines. Three years later he purchased another 10 hectares (25 acres) and began experimenting with growing French hybrids and vinifera. He enrolled at Cornell University for additional condensed courses in professional winemaking. Now the owner of 14 hectares (35 acres) of excellent, sandy/clay soil, located close to Niagara-on-the-Lake, Joe decided to apply his knowledge as a self-taught winemaker and his skills as an engineer to build a winery. He named his winery Newark Winery after the village of Newark, which was chosen by Lieutenant-Governor John Graves Simcoe as the first capital of Upper Canada, and that later became the town of Niagara-on-the-Lake.

From the beginning, Joe Pohorly took great pains to produce quality wines. He used stainless-steel tanks to produce his white wines and wooden vats for his reds. For the first two years the bottling was done by Inniskillin Winery. From the start Newark Winery was a true family affair. Betty, Joe's wife, became the company's treasurer, and their three daughters helped in the vineyard and in the winery store.

To honor his wife, Joe named his first rosé wine Elizabeth Rose. The white blend Lady Ann was named for his wife and three daughters, as all of them had Ann as their middle name. Newark's red wine, Maréchal Foch, became Chevalier Rouge, and a white blend Comtesse Blanche. Joe's decision to grow French hybrids and vinifera had been amply justified. He began to experiment with such varieties as Mario Muscat, Chardonnay, Pinot Noir, Pinot Blanc and Riesling. Newark's 1980 Gewürztraminer was praised for its outstanding quality. Together with the 1981 Chardonnay and Johannisberg Riesling, they were listed in the Toronto Rare Wine Store. The Liquor Control Board of Ontario stores also carried a number of his wines.

Joe told us some of this history as we toured the winery that day. He and Betty were warm and hospitable and we enjoyed listening to their stories. The equipment was very simple, more or less the same as we had seen at Château des Charmes. There was one distinct difference. Joe showed us a small stainless-steel tank wrapped with rubber hoses and attached to a water tap. There were also wires leading to a computer. He explained that this was a preliminary experiment being conducted by two professors from the University of Guelph, Dr. Anthony Meiering, who had already experimented in microprocessors in the field of fermentation, and Dr. Ron Subden, professor of microbiology.

The researchers, Joe told us, believed that they would be able to find a new method of improving the quality of Ontario wines by regulating the temperature with computer sensors. These computer sensors would adjust temperature levels automatically during the wine fermentation and would also give an accurate reading of the natural sugar levels in the juice. After several meetings to determine the possibilities and requirements of applying this method for commercial-scale application, the National Research Council of Canada had approved partial funding for a two-year research project.

Emil Underberg was most interested in these experiments. His company had been working closely with university professors in Germany to develop new methods to make his products almost histamine-free, that is, free of allergenic impurities. So he had firsthand positive experience with research projects.

After touring the winery Joe took us to his vineyards, where he had set up experimental plots of European hybrids. These consisted of Seyval Blanc, Vidal, Baco Noir, Maréchal Foch and an early North American hybrid, Duchess, in addition to vinifera varieties, which included Chardonnay and Gewürztraminer grapes. He explained that the Gewürztraminer vines were extremely frost-tender, and to protect them from the severe cold, he had to prune them back each fall and bury them for the winter. They then had to be uncovered and retrained in the spring. This triggered old memories, for me, of our gardener in Poland, who would protect small fig trees in the same way, except that he would first cover them with straw and then soil.

After our tour of the vineyards Joe invited us to his wine store for a tasting. We found the Gewürztraminer to be an exciting wine, with an intensely distinctive nose and a spicy flavor with a touch of bitterness. After the tasting we proceeded to Joe's home, where Betty was waiting for us with coffee.

While we were enjoying their hospitality, Joe explained why he and Betty had decided to look for a suitable partner to assure a promising future for Newark Winery. The winery needed a dynamic expansion to become a top-quality estates winery (a winery that produces and bottles its own wine on its own property), but with the steadily increasing interest rates, Joe could not afford to raise enough capital. We appreciated his straightforward approach and, at the same time, his conviction that this was the right time to invest in the business. He also gave us some interesting news about the local growers. Paul Bosc, Karl Kaiser, Donald Ziraldo and Joe had made great efforts to shift the Canadian wine industry away from the Labrusca grapes toward premium hybrids and vinifera. They had started to convince local grape growers to change to these grape varieties, in anticipation of future demand.

Emil was pleased with his visit to Newark Winery and our meeting with Joe and Betty Pohorly. During lunch at the Prince of Wales restaurant, we all agreed that this was the winery we had been looking for, especially as Joe Pohorly was willing to sell the majority of his ownership and stay on as the manager. We arranged to meet our lawyer, David Nathanson, early in the morning to prepare an offer to the Pohorlys and to discuss the details to be covered in the final agreement.

On our way back to Toronto we stopped at Newark Winery to inform Joe and Betty Pohorly about our decision and tell them that the offer would be forthcoming. The adventure had begun.

3

NEW BEGINNINGS—
THE INVESTMENT BEGINS

*E*mil Underberg returned to Germany. As a result of the ensuing negotiations, 61.7 percent of Newark Winery was acquired by the Underberg Company on September 3, 1982. Joe Pohorly owned 33.3 percent of the shares and Robert Mielzynski owned the other 5 percent. I was appointed as chairman and Joe Pohorly as president. At the same time, Peter Mielzynski Agencies was named the official sales agent to represent Newark's products. Newark became a sister company of Scholl and Hillebrand, in the Rhine region in Germany, and Schlumberger, in Vienna, Austria. Consequently, Newark Winery was able to draw upon many generations of winemaking experience and tradition. Bernhard Breuer and Heinz Turk were designated as special wine consultants to Newark. Newark's future looked secure. It was now part of the Underberg group of companies, which gave it a range of resources to draw on.

Soon after the deal was signed with the Underberg Company, Peter Mielzynski Agencies took over the promotion of all Newark Winery brands. Their wines were already listed by the LCBO, but it was up to individual stores to make their own selection from that list. Our goal was to introduce the wines to as many LCBO stores as possible in order to generate interest with prospective customers. Another important market was the restaurant trade. Although a few restaurants already offered some of our products, to make it onto more wine lists Newark needed a good-quality table wine, bottled in two sizes—1-liter (34-oz.) and 1.5-liter (51-oz.). We made this one of our top priorities.

Heinz Turk and Helmuth van Schellenbeck, a director of the Underberg Company in Switzerland, traveled from Europe to assist us in the planning process. The areas of discussion were far-ranging. First and foremost we needed to find and hire a highly qualified winemaker, with roots in the European tradition of winemaking. We also needed new equipment to improve the production process, and we needed to identify and approach grape growers who could share our vision. Moreover, we needed buildings to accommodate the new large fermentation and storage tanks. Then, of course, we had to introduce new brands onto the Ontario market as quickly as possible.

Before we started to plan activities for 1983 we reviewed our long-term goal—to become the "top producer of world-class wines in Canada." We also took stock of our situation. There was limited availability of varietal grapes in the Niagara region. The varietals that were being grown were sold to Inniskillin Winery and Château des Charmes, with only small amounts going to some of the large wineries. Consequently, Newark Winery, at least for the first three years, would have only hybrid grapes to work with. That would limit us to producing mainly house wines.

As a result of our deliberations we decided to add a new cellar for large fermentation tanks and to provide the winery with the most modern equipment and top technical assistance. These innovations would allow us to immediately produce table wines equal to the imported table wines from Europe, even though we had access to only hybrid grapes. At the same time we decided to develop a medium- to long-term research plan. Another key ingredient of our vision was to educate and support growers to make the switch to selected varietal grapes.

Technical assistance took many forms. In 1983, Joe Pohorly and his assistant, Peter Gamble, were joined by a new oenologist (wine-maker), Jurgen Helbig, graduate of the famous Geisenheim School of Oenology, located in Germany. Meanwhile, Heinz Turk and Bernhard Breuer selected the much-needed modern equipment, which was purchased in Europe.

The new investments in the Newark Winery were timely since, according to the latest report from the Canadian Wine Institute, Ontarians were drinking more wine than ever before. In 1977, the average per capita wine consumption was 6.19 liters (206 oz.), but by 1982 it had climbed to 8.49 liters (283 oz.). And consumers were beginning to develop a taste for local wines. In March 1977, 56 domestic wines were listed with the LCBO. Five years later this had risen to 146. White wines accounted for a large proportion of the consumption of both domestic and imported wines.

I conducted a research study of the Ontario market and found that the Newark name was not well known and that the public did not associate it with the Niagara wine region. Since we were planning to introduce German-type wines in 1983, we decided to find a name that would convey a sense of tradition and a connection to a European wine heritage. We chose the name Hillebrand. Our sister company, Scholl and Hillebrand, was more than a century old, and the Rheingau, where the winery was located, was the best-known grape-growing area in Germany.

In keeping with our name change and given consumers' sweeter tastes, I proposed that the first German-style wine be called Schloss Hillebrand. The name was very well accepted by our group. We notified Bernhard Breuer of the results of our meetings and asked him to come in January to oversee the blending of the new wine.

There was not much time to develop a good promotional package for Schloss Hillebrand. During my previous trip to Germany I had collected many wine labels so as to give us some ideas to work from when creating a suitable label for our new wine. My approach, developed over years in the business, is that a label should both inform the customers and draw their attention to the product.

I contacted Bill Jodek, Toronto representative for Montreal's Jonergin Company, specialists in label production. Bill, who had become a personal friend, had worked with me when I was at McGuinness Distillery. After poring over my collection of labels, he devised a few designs for Schloss Hillebrand. This was only the beginning. The proposed mock-up label was placed on bottles, as a test run, at some LCBO stores. After corrections and many redesigning efforts, the Jonergin Company was given the green light to print and emboss the label; it had Germanic-style gothic lettering and a view of the Rhineland countryside in the background—and perfectly portrayed the character of the wine. We were delighted with the final product.

Meanwhile, Joe Pohorly, Bernhard Breuer and Heinz Turk had been using a combination of technical expertise and artistic flair to create the right blend for Schloss Hillebrand. The wine was pale, straw-yellow in color, with a pronounced but attractive honey-flowery bouquet and a hint of spicy sweetness in the taste, ideal for summer drinking. At $7.10 for a 1.5-liter (51-oz.) bottle and $4.60 for a 750-mL (25-oz.) bottle, Schloss Hillebrand attracted price-conscious customers, and the handsome, Bordeaux-style magnum bottle, with an impressive label, caught the attention of wine buyers.

The residual sugar (the amount of natural sugar remaining in the wine at the time of bottling) for Schloss Hillebrand was #2. The residual sugar was harmonized with the acidity and this made Schloss Hillebrand a very well balanced wine. Indeed, Tony Aspler, wine critic for the *Toronto Star*, described the Schloss thus: "It had an intense floral bouquet with a ripe, sweet taste. . . . the wine is clean and round with good length and finish. . . . a real winemaker's wine."

In 1983 we launched Schloss Hillebrand on the Ontario market. The timing was perfect; Canadian white wines were outselling Canadian reds by three to one, and German-style white wines were very popular. This was a period during which German wines, such as Sichel's Blue Nun, sold 120,000 cases a year. Schloss Hillebrand became an immediate success.

In the meantime, Joe Pohorly had put the finishing touches on his plans for building a new cellar and accompanying laboratories. A number of 20,000-liter (5,200-gallon) capacity tanks had been ordered from Italy, as well as a brand-new receiving hopper. This equipment would be essential during the harvest, to cope with the winery's increased production.

Plans were also under way to produce a pair of French-type table wines. Le Baron Blanc and Le Baron Rouge were to be launched on the market in the fall of 1983. Joe Pohorly prepared samples of different blends for the new wines. Bernhard Breuer, assisted by our new winemaker, Jurgen Helbig, his associate winemaker, Peter Gamble, and Adrian Williamson, our wine expert from Peter Mielzynski Agencies, tasted a variety of blends to determine which would best meet the critical demands of the consumer. And there were laboratory tests. All blends prepared for bottling had to be analyzed for quality control by the Underberg Research Laboratories in Zurich.

Peter Mielzynski Agencies' representatives were under a good deal of pressure. In order to successfully launch Le Baron Blanc and Le Baron Rouge, Schloss Hillebrand had to be first listed in as many stores as possible. The Hillebrand name was still new to the consumer, and the Peter Mielzynski Agencies' representatives had to build brand awareness. One of the ways they did this was through Schloss Hillebrand tastings, mainly in small communities and cottage areas, where we had noticed that Schloss sales were brisk.

The agency produced a newsletter, edited by Adrian Williamson, called *Notes from Peter's Cellar*. It proved to be very useful in promoting Hillebrand wines. Adrian had a good sense of consumer tastes and trends, and he was knowledgeable about both local and imported wines. Indeed, he was one of the team who provided input in developing new Hillebrand wines. As wine consumption in Ontario was on the increase, so was consumer interest in how wines and spirits were made. The newsletter was a strategic way of catering to that interest and building customer loyalty.

Sales representatives encouraged customers to visit the Hillebrand Winery and discover the grape-growing area of Niagara-on-the-Lake. Joe Pohorly was very appreciative of these efforts. He noticed a great increase in the number of visitors to the winery coming from all parts of the province.

Joe had always believed in the team spirit and wanted to celebrate the satisfying success of the winery. He and Betty invited all the Peter Mielzynski Agencies' representatives and their spouses, together with the Hillebrand employees, to a garden party at their home in 1983. He also invited a few grape growers to join the party. At the party Joe thanked the sales representatives for doing such a good job of promoting and distributing Hillebrand wines, and for their efforts in putting the Niagara region on the map. He also announced that his associate winemaker, Peter Gamble, was being promoted to a newly created position of production manager and would be working very closely with Jurgen Helbig.

Peter Mielzynski Agencies' strategy of heavily promoting Schloss Hillebrand before Le Baron Blanc and Le Baron Rouge were introduced paid off. Schloss Hillebrand paved the way for these new wines. Le Baron Blanc was a dry white wine, with good acidity and a fresh, crisp flavor, a very well blended wine. Le Baron Rouge was blended to meet the demand for a light, Beaujolais-style, fruity wine that would complement meat dishes as well as cheeses. The very elegant labels, designed and produced by Jonergin Company, could not be missed. Adrian Williamson commented in *Notes from Peter's Cellar* that "to Bernhard Breuer blending wines is like an artist working on a painting. One has to visualise in advance the message to be conveyed and the subtle influence of each component grape type. The marriage of artistic temperament and technical details contributes to the making of well-balanced wine."

Emil Underberg, owner of Hillebrand Estates Winery, strongly believed in the potential of the Niagara Region to become an internationally recognized wine-producing area.

Author Peter Mielzynski-Zychlinski, chairman of Hillebrand Estates Winery, was convinced, from the beginning, of the future success of the Hillebrand venture. He envisioned the Niagara Region as an important, flourishing area proud of its Canadian wine culture.

Joe Pohorly, the first president of Hillebrand Estates Winery. In 1965, he was already a pioneer in growing French hybrids and vinifera grapes in the Niagara-on-the-Lake area.

Scott Moore, production manager of Hillebrand Estates Winery, made an invaluable contribution to the winery.

Benoit (Ben) Huchin (right), master winemaker, tasting excellent Hillebrand wines with Jean Laurent Groux, the assistant winemaker.

Niagara grape growers under contract with Hillebrand display signs specifying that their grapes were grown exclusively for our winery.

(left) John Watson, grape grower and loyal supplier to Hillebrand Estates Winery.

(right) Albrecht Seeger, grape grower, is one of the most successful pioneers in cultivating classical varietal grapes.

Matthias Oppenlaender, the very successful manager of Huebel Estates Vineyards, which supplied Hillebrand Estates Winery with excellent varietal grapes.

Three generations of the Buis Family, ambitious growers of Glenlake Vineyards. They were very successful in growing classical varietal grapes as early as 1980.

Jack Forrier, grape grower, strongly believed in the Niagara region's potential for vinifera grapes.

From left to right: Klaus Reif, Ewald Reif's nephew; Ewald Reif and Peter D. Mielzynski. Ewald started his vineyard in 1977 and became a pioneer grower of world-class grapes. When he later built his own winery, his nephew Klaus joined him as a winemaker.

Hillebrand Estates Winery's outstanding viticulturist, Greg Berti.

Bernhard Breuer, wine consultant to Hillebrand Estates Winery and descendant of seven generations of wine producers who owned Scholl & Hillebrand Winery in Germany.

It was at Bernhard Breuer's insistence that Hillebrand Winery started, in late 1983, to produce Eiswein (which literally means "Icewine") using European hybrids. Eiswein is made, in the old German tradition, by leaving the grapes on the vine rather than harvesting them in the early autumn. Usually, grapes are harvested in September or early October, but the ones selected for Eiswein are netted to protect them from birds, while waiting for the desired cold weather, which normally arrives in December or January. As the grapes continue to ripen, the sugar levels increase. Once the temperature drops to between −8° and −15°C (18° and 5°F) for five consecutive days, the water inside the grapes causes them to crystallize. That's when the grapes are picked by hand and put into a manually operated press. The pickers often work through the night, usually between midnight and 8:00 a.m., when the air is the coldest, to prevent the ice crystals from melting into juice. Each grape produces a few drops of the precious sweet nectar.

Sadly, our winemaker, Jurgen Helbig, had to leave Hillebrand and return to Germany shortly after the harvest and pressing of the frozen Vidal grapes for the production of Hillebrand's first Eiswein. He had done an excellent job in developing our new wines in 1983, and he had helped Hillebrand become the first Ontario winery to supply Eiswein to the LCBO speciality stores and Ontario customers.

Introducing Eiswein for the first time created a challenge for Peter Gamble. In addition to finding an increased supply of grapes for Schloss Hillebrand, Le Baron Blanc and Le Baron Rouge, he now also had to find a good source of Vidal grapes. And the grape growers would have to be familiarized with the procedures required in the making of Eiswein. The winery had to estimate the volume of grapes to be left on the vine and picked in December or January, come to an agreement with the grower and pay ahead of time. There were risks and the winery assumed them all, the weather being one. If there was too much rain, the quality of grapes would be adversely affected. Even with nets, flocks of birds could destroy the crop, since once the leaves were shed the grapes were exposed. And these grapes are often harvested in very difficult weather conditions. But the harvest had its own magic. Hillebrand organized a bonfire and provided hot drinks and food for the pickers.

When Emil Underberg bought Newark Winery, his idea was not to emulate the big wineries. He was not after high volume. His goal was to develop the winery to produce premium-quality wines. We were all determined to reach this goal. From the beginning, our consultant, Bernhard Breuer, insisted that "to make sound wines, a narrow concentrated focus is better than a digressive and diluted one. Rather than opt for a wide range of wines, Hillebrand Estates should limit itself, for the time being, to several blends and three or four varietals." Heinz Turk and Joe Pohorly agreed wholeheartedly with Bernhard, and from 1983 to 1986 focused on developing the appropriate grape varieties.

In collaboration with the Rhine-Danube Research Station and Leamington Euro Nurseries in Leamington, Ontario, Bernhard Breuer and Joe Pohorly chose only the grapes best suited to the Niagara area. A rigorous selection process was implemented to obtain high-quality strains of Riesling, Chardonnay, Pinot Blanc and certain hybrid grapes to begin the development of the experimental vineyard at Hillebrand and the vineyards of the contract growers.

On the advice of our advisers, Heinz Turk and Helmuth van Schellenbeck, we agreed to follow the European-quality system by attaching two very important conditions to our grape growers. First, the harvest date had to be determined by our winemaker, as this decision dictated the quality of the wine. The correct harvest date was critical. It is possible to create superior-quality wines only when the grapes are picked at the optimum moment of maturity, with sugar and acid balance appropriate to the wine being produced. The second condition was that the grapes had to be delivered to the winery for processing immediately after being picked. In order to ensure that there were no delays at our end, we had installed a brand-new, state-of-the-art receiving hopper so that the grapes could be unloaded quickly and efficiently.

Hillebrand's existing growers were initially reluctant to consider this new approach to viticulture. As the year went on, however, they could see that we were committed to the future of the wine industry, and their enthusiasm grew. The grape growers had not experienced such commitment from a winery. Previously they had always been uncertain, right up to the harvest date, as to whether or not their crop would be purchased. Thanks to Peter Gamble and Joe Pohorly's positive relationship with the grape growers, the growers finally recognized that the conditions we were insisting on were mutually beneficial. This, in turn, improved their understanding and cooperation with Hillebrand, and soon, new grape growers became interested in coming on board.

We were happy with Hillebrand's progress in 1983. Sales in the Ontario market had almost quadrupled, from 4,500 cases in 1982 to 15,200. And Schloss Hillebrand and Le Baron Blanc and Rouge had secured a lot of attention. Schloss Hillebrand earned a Best of Class medal at the 1983 International Eastern Wine Competition in New York. The Gewürztraminer won Top Ontario Wine at the 1983 *Windsor Star* Tasting, and it was a double medal winner at the 1983 International Eastern Wine Competition, which boasted over 700 entries. Such recognition of the quality of wines from Hillebrand in our first year provided us with the knowledge and enthusiasm for the future.

4

FULL STEAM AHEAD

*I*f 1983 had shown us anything it was that quality grapes and technical know-how make for better wines. The next step was to purchase the Europress—a first in Canada. It was an expensive piece of equipment, but simply the best. It worked this way: Imagine a balloon being inflated inside a drum. The grapes were pressed against the side of a perforated, revolving drum by a large bag that was inflated pneumatically. This is called a soft press. Normal presses crush the grapes, which can cause a bitter taste from the broken seeds of the grape. The Europress's gentle process left the seeds intact, producing a free-run juice untainted by tannin, an astringent substance. With the new Europress we could expect an immediate improvement in the quality of our wine.

Another piece of equipment the Underberg Company purchased was a de-stemmer/crusher. This machine allowed the Europress to function properly by removing the grape stalks before pressing. After de-stemming, the white grape-must, newly pressed juices of grapes ready for fermentation, was pumped directly to the stainless-steel fermentation tank. The red grape-must was directed to an open-topped, stainless-steel fermentation tank, where cultured yeast was added. During the four to seven days of fermentation, the skins continually rose and formed a stiff, thick cap on the surface of the wine. In order to extract color and flavor from the skins, wine from the bottom of the tank was "pumped over" the skins. After fermentation, the wine-drenched skins were put through the Europress again to extract the remaining red wine, rich in color.

The purchase and installation of the de-stemmer/crusher and the Europress was a costly investment for Emil Underberg. However, this new procedure, unknown until then in Canada, would assure Hillebrand Winery the purest juice from which to produce clean, well-balanced wines.

Both machines were delivered and installed before the start of the 1984 harvest tourist season. Hillebrand Estates Winery had been transformed into a modern, well-equipped winery, and we wanted people to observe firsthand our state-of-the-art winemaking process. Winery tours, presented by Joe Pohorly's two enthusiastic daughters, included free wine tastings. Joe's philosophy was "seeing is believing."

Peter Mielzynski Agencies' representatives also invited many LCBO personnel to visit Hillebrand. The representatives also organized wine tastings across Ontario, introducing the Hillebrand wines alongside imported wines. Moreover, they encouraged their customers, who were planning to visit Niagara, to include Hillebrand Estates Winery in their agenda. And every year the agency organized boat tours, inviting restaurant owners and beverage managers, together with their families, to a relaxing outing to enjoy our wine tastings.

Other positive influences were also at work. The annual Shaw Festival helped promote the restoration and redevelopment of the Niagara-on-the-Lake region. Hillebrand Winery attracted Shaw Festival visitors who were keen to learn about the latest advances in Ontario wine production.

At the beginning of 1984, the new winemaker, Andreas Gestaltner, arrived. Andreas was a young man who had trained in Austria at the Wine Institute of Schlumberger. He was the right person to join our team at that time. He had a creative approach to the art of winemaking, which was a great plus for Hillebrand, since we were committed to introducing a new wine culture to the Niagara region. Andreas and Heinz Turk arrived just as we were in the process of developing our bicentennial wines.

The Ontario government had established a bicentennial committee to oversee the province's celebrations. One of the committee's many goals for the historic occasion was that it be marked by the creation of special Ontario-made wines. Of all the wineries approached, Hillebrand was the only one who decided to accept the challenge—to vint a new wine to celebrate Ontario's 200-year history.

We looked for a suitable name for our bicentennial vintage and decided to call it Étienne Brûlé, in memory of one of Ontario's early explorers. Ontario artist Marie Hands was commissioned to design the label depicting the province's flower, the trillium. The official bicentennial seal Celebrating Together was an elegant addition to the charming design.

Now we had to make our selection for the bicentennial wine from several blends of red and white wines. A panel of tasters, led by Heinz Turk, tasted and debated for quite some time before they made their final decision. The outcome of this enjoyable selection process was Étienne Brûlé Rouge, a soft red wine, with a fruitiness in its taste, a wonderful fragrance and a fully satisfying finish, and Étienne Brûlé Blanc, a dry, fruity, savory, blond wine, with an elegant character and a firm fresh taste.

Hillebrand succeeded in getting a commitment from the LCBO to list Étienne Brûlé Blanc and Rouge in 450 stores as soon as it became available for shipment. This was a great opportunity to showcase the Hillebrand name to consumers across the province. At the same time, the LCBO organized a special bicentennial display in the stores, together with distinctive celebration posters. Other local wineries that had affixed the bicentennial logo onto their regular wines also participated in these displays.

Hillebrand created attractive duo presentation packages including both bicentennial wines. These were given as gifts by the provincial government to special guests visiting Ontario for the bicentennial celebrations. These were also available in Hillebrand's two stores.

Our reward came when Norman Best, executive director of the bicentennial committee, declared Étienne Brûlé Rouge and Étienne Brûlé Blanc to be the official bicentennial wines for Ontario. In June we organized a party to officially launch the brands. Attending was the deputy premier of Ontario, Margaret Birch, who was also the chairperson of the bicentennial committee, Norman Best, Jack Ackroyd, chairman of the LCBO, and several ministers of the provincial government. We were also joined by Hillebrand's newly appointed vice president of marketing and development, John Swan.

The Étienne Brûlé wines became so successful that Norman Best allowed us to continue to use the official bicentennial logo for its subsequent vintages.

In February 1984, John Swan was hired as a special representative for the Underberg brands represented by Peter Mielzynski Agencies. John came from the United Kingdom, where he had considerable experience in the wine trade. He had worked for six years for the leading supermarket group Tesco, developing their retail wine distribution. In the seven years before immigrating to Canada, he had been the managing director of the German Pieroth, a large winery located in Rhineland, in charge of their French wine division in the United Kingdom. John Swan had the right qualifications and experience to open and develop high-image wine stores in Ontario, which was what the Hillebrand Winery wanted.

Later that year we decided to open our first store outside the winery, called Hillebrand. After researching the possibilities, John chose an excellent location, in the College Park Plaza in Toronto, almost next door to the subway station entrance. There were many offices in College Park and the neighboring area, and it was a high-traffic zone, particularly during morning and afternoon rush hours. We quickly developed a customer base. We did not yet have a great selection of varietal wines to offer customers, but our main objective, at that time, was to create customer awareness of the Hillebrand Estates Winery.

As Peter Mielzynski Agencies' office was just a short walk from the store, I would often go over and spend time with the customers, getting a sense of their preferences and buying habits. I enjoyed it. Indeed I would spend the occasional Saturday at the store, selling wines and talking to customers.

I discovered that many young people were open-minded about trying Ontario wines. More mature customers, who were accustomed to drinking imported wines, were much more conservative and resistant to trying domestic wines. One had to be particularly persuasive with these customers to get them to try a Hillebrand wine that approximated the taste of their favorite imported wine. My sales experiences convinced me that our next store should be located in a more residential shopping area, close to delicatessens and gourmet cheese stores. The area I had in mind was Toronto's Bloor West Village, which attracted shoppers who came from other parts of the city. We opened our second store there, shortly after opening our first.

I had great faith in the future of our stores, but we needed to work to give the grape growers the confidence and conviction that their success depended on producing world-class grapes. At Hillebrand, we realized that before we expanded the number of stores, we had to have a greater variety of products. That meant partnering with more grape growers who could produce the best-quality varietal grapes.

In July 1984 we had another timely visit from Bernhard Breuer. We prepared a tasting of our Hillebrand Eiswein, which had been produced based on his recommendations during his 1983 visit. The supply was limited, as is usually the case, but in Bernhard's opinion the wine could be favorably compared to the traditionally produced Eiswein of Germany. It was presented in 375-mL (13-oz.) bottles with a very attractive label and would be the first domestically produced Eiswein to be sold through LCBO stores.

Since we were certain to have competition in the future from other estate wineries, Peter Gamble had already arranged with several of our Vidal grape growers to be available for our 1984 Eiswein production.

The years 1983 and 1984 marked the completion of our short-term plans for Hillebrand. The new cellar was added to the original winery, the most modern equipment was installed and a wide range of wines was introduced to the Ontario market with remarkable success.

During 1984, Hillebrand Estates Winery sold 26,292 cases through the LCBO outlets alone. We won the silver medal and the Best of Class Award for Schloss Hillebrand at the 1984 International Eastern Wine Competition in New York. At the same competition, Hillebrand's 1983 vintage Eiswein was awarded the bronze and our Étienne Brûlé Rouge earned an honorable mention. At the 1984 International Wine and Spirit Competition in the United Kingdom, Hillebrand's 1982 vintage Gewürztraminer won the bronze medal.

Hillebrand Estates Winery hosted thousands of visitors from across Ontario that year, many of them encouraged to visit the winery by Peter Mielzynski Agencies' representatives. We noted an increase in consumer interest in the art of winemaking. As the number of visitors increased, we made plans to expand our facilities to include a video screening room where we gave visitors an overview of the process of winemaking.

Following the initial success of our College Park and Bloor West Village retail outlets, we embarked on a plan to develop a network of stores in strategic locations throughout Ontario. We wanted the stores to provide our customers with the full range of varietal, sparkling and table wines. Our aim was to become the local wine merchant, an extension of the winery, where customers would enjoy not only the products but also the service and information provided.

We submitted our 1985–86 feasibility plan to Emil Underberg with a view of further enlarging the winery facilities, stressing the importance of having a large area for the tour groups we expected. In the same submission, we proposed to establish five new stores in 1985 and seven more a year later.

Immediately after our plans were approved, John Swan started to look for the most advantageous markets and specific locations for the five additional stores. He visited many LCBO stores to review their wine sales and to derive a clear profile of the clientele. He spent time in large malls in order to gauge residential demographics and purchasing power. John also visited food stores and boutiques and checked pedestrian and vehicular traffic, as well as local parking, facilities. Peter Mielzynski Agencies' representatives assisted with market research, as they knew the potential of the wine sales in their areas.

Toward the end of 1985, Hillebrand Winery opened five more stores, located in London, Hamilton, Clarkson, Oakville and The Beaches area in Toronto. John introduced short- and long-term educational programs for the store managers and clerks. These programs focused on knowledge of the wines themselves, public relations and store display. Staff were provided with training in how to manage the store and how to be the public face for the winery. In addition, there were in-depth programs taught by Peter Gamble. These classes highlighted the different kinds of grapes grown in the Niagara-on-the-Lake region and included systematic visits to the farms of the grape growers. Our winemaker, Andreas Gestaltner, explained the production of wine to our new employees and taught them how to organize simple but informative wine tastings. People hired to work in our stores had to work hard, do a lot of homework and go through extensive written tests before they became Hillebrand wine merchants.

Meanwhile, at the winery, Joe Pohorly proved to be a versatile executive who was able to build an excellent team of dedicated employees. It was a difficult task to meet the increased demand from both the

LCBO and our own stores. Demand for Hillebrand wines almost outstripped our ability to supply. It was only through the quality of our staff and their ingenuity that we were able to deliver wines on time.

Every aspect of the process had to work efficiently. In 1985, our bottling line consisted of a small 12-spout mono block filler and bottle corker, and a small labeler capable of doing front labels only. The bottling line production capacity was 30,000 cases a year. Scott Moore, a versatile employee who had been promoted from maintenance work to managing the bottling line, was able to upgrade the line several times before a new one was installed.

From 1983 to 1985, Underberg's investments in Hillebrand Winery were over $3.5 million. This amount would have been much higher had it not been for the fine work of many dedicated employees.

We were all thrilled with the excellent results of our wine sales in our stores during the first six months of 1985. The winery store sales had increased by 61 percent and the College Park store by 42 percent over the previous year. Later in the year the newly opened stores in Hamilton, Oakville, London and Clarkson racked up impressive sales, but The Beaches' store sales were stellar, averaging $3,500 a week for the first month.

During the first three months of 1986, five more stores were opened. Prospective managers were hired for each store, and extensive training was started. John Swan came up with a novel plan for the stores, which would make them profit centers by May 1986. The managers would receive incentives based on the sales and profitability of their stores. This system would encourage them to generate more outside business. At the same time, educational programs for clerks and managers would continue in the form of correspondence courses and field training. Every three months the staff would be tested, and, if successful, they would receive a certificate of accomplishment at the end of the 12-month period. Any staff member not interested in participating would have no future in our retail stores. The proposed plan was approved. It helped Hillebrand to develop quality sales personnel while also emphasizing the relationship between education and sales.

The cost of opening each store, together with the training of new staff, was $25,000. It was an expensive and risky business, but if successful would provide a healthier cash flow and future profits. According to our plan, we would have 20 stores in operation by the end of 1987. They would generate sales of between $3.8 to $4 million a year.

Our concept of bringing the image of the winery to the stores through education, and in turn inviting our customers to the winery, was working. This provided us with the incentive to continue with more stores.

5

ONTARIO WINES COME OF AGE

*E*very aspect of the Hillebrand Winery was growing in 1986. Hillebrand urgently required considerable new investments from the shareholders, the Underberg Company and Joe Pohorly. It was Underberg policy to manage and operate its subsidiaries, including Hillebrand Estates Winery, so that they would always be in a position to meet their financial and other obligations. From the beginning, the Niagara Credit Union Bank in Niagara-on-the-Lake had been our bankers. Discussions in 1986 with the credit union were under way to increase our line of credit for future growth. As usual they were most helpful and understanding. Unfortunately, however, they couldn't offer the range of services Hillebrand now required. For example, with our growing number of stores, we needed a multibranch financial institution so that our store managers could make daily deposits. We started to review other options in the banking world.

I was a member of the Goodwood Club, a fishing and hunting club, and one of my fellow members was Doug Gardiner, vice chairman of the Royal Bank of Canada. I discussed the problem with him and he, in turn, reviewed the situation with D. R. McLennan, manager of the

Royal Bank in St. Catharines. The bank was very interested in Hillebrand. They indicated that they were prepared to provide needed funds during the expansion of the business, but they wanted to see equity injection by the shareholders. The willingness of the Royal Bank to take on our business was a symbol of corporate confidence in Hillebrand Estates Winery; perhaps even more so because the Royal, at that time, had the reputation for being very conservative. We now had behind us two great powers: the successful German industrialist Emil Underberg and the Royal Bank of Canada.

The local grape growers were also taking a keen interest in the development of the winery. Never before had they seen such a firm commitment to local grapes and the marketing of Ontario wines. It was exciting to witness the turning point in the growers' confidence in Hillebrand. News of the Royal Bank's backing further increased the grape growers' optimism for the future.

At that time there were no real in-depth viticulture education and training programs in Canada. We felt it was important to build a knowledge base. As partners of the growers, we decided to invite viticulture experts from around the world to come to Canada to educate us. We also wanted to find someone who would be accessible to us on a regular basis.

We needed someone educated in viticulture, who would be able to study and work with the growers on establishing a program for planting vinifera grape vines in suitable areas of the Niagara region, taking into account soil types and climatic conditions. Our friend from Guelph University, Dr. Ron Subden, who taught wine basics, had highly recommended one of his students, Greg Berti. Originally, Greg had wanted to study viticulture, but as courses in this field were not available he decided to study horticulture instead, since the two sciences were closely related. However, his interest in viticulture did not wane, and he enrolled in Professor Subden's wine basics courses.

Greg had two more years at the university, but the faculty at Guelph agreed that he could study for four months and work the rest of the year in the field of viticulture, at Hillebrand. This valuable experience would be credited to his university program. Greg made a very positive impression on Joe Pohorly and John Swan during his interview. His commitment to experimenting with new varieties of grapes was particularly striking. Greg's motto was "There should always be room for the innovators," and that suited Hillebrand. Greg was hired from April to December 1985, with an understanding that the same arrangement would be in place for 1986.

Joe Pohorly marked out a program for Greg to plant new Vidal vines for the Eiswein production at Hillebrand. The program also included experiments with various trellising systems in the vineyards. Peter Gamble introduced him to the grape growers with whom he would be working closely. Soon, Greg's careful observations enabled him to track the different climatic conditions between Niagara and Guelph.

Greg had an opportunity to learn the art of winemaking from Andreas Gestaltner. He also came to appreciate Hillebrand's state-of-the-art equipment. He soon discovered that the only missing ingredient in Hillebrand's growth plan was better-quality grapes. It was this that would allow the winery to produce superior wines. Through viticultural science Greg planned to cultivate a better quality of grapes. At the same time he saw the need to experiment with new varieties that might be introduced to the region.

Increased sales and an extraordinary harvest made 1985 Hillebrand's best year. With the bumper harvest, we purchased grapes at a cost of approximately $450,000. In order to meet production demands, a number of stainless-steel tanks with a 228,000-liter (60,000-gallon) capacity had to be installed.

As expected, in 1985, 6,000 cases of varietal wines were purchased by our stores and the LCBO. This was a large increase over the previous year. We could, within two years, expect to become number one in sales of varietal wines in Ontario. A rigorous planting schedule was agreed upon in order to meet projected demand. Based on input from Peter Mielzynski Agencies, the winery expected an increase of 21 percent in the LCBO stores' listings on existing and newly developed products.

And we had entered a new market: We received the first order from Air Canada for our Maréchal Foch. Air Canada selected wines using strict quality controls and a tasting panel. Over 200,000 187-mL (6-oz.) bottles were consumed in the first year by Air Canada passengers. This was excellent exposure for Hillebrand. We printed a special back label for the bottles, not only with a description of the wine, but also with an invitation to visit the winery. Many of our visitors mentioned that they had first learned about Hillebrand Estates Winery flying at 32,000 feet!

While varietal wines were the main thrust of Hillebrand's future, good-quality house wines were also part of the strategy to provide a full selection to the consumer. In 1985, the bag-in-the-box format, an idea that originated in Australia, was adopted at Hillebrand for the convenience of customers wanting wine on tap. However, we were not happy with the 4-liter (135-oz.) box format available at that time. It was too large for storage in the refrigerator and it was also heavy. We researched other options and found a manufacturer who produced a 3-liter (101-oz.) size that was easier to handle and would fit in the door of the refrigerator. Our first 3-liter (101-oz.) box, the Étienne Brûlé, was an instant success.

At the opposite end of the spectrum we developed a private label program. Through our stores we were able to establish direct contact with our customers, which provided us with opportunities not available to wineries that sold through only the LCBO. We found that both our corporate and private customers were interested in a service not found elsewhere—private labels. Hence a private wine-labeling program was created. This offered companies the chance to show their names and logos on wine served at special functions or given as gifts. For more personal events, such as a wedding, customers could serve their "own" wine, with their name on the label.

As we added products and services, we were also adding to our list of wines. Hillebrand introduced a number of exciting new products.

Peterhof was a dry, German-style wine, with a distinct floral aroma and a fresh, intriguing taste. Reasonably priced, it was a wonderful example of the new-style "trocken"—the German word for dry. For those preferring their wine more in the French style, another release, Hillebrand Canadian Chablis, was created. Dry and full-bodied, this white wine repeatedly outscored both domestic and imported Chablis in blind tastings. Demand was such that we decided to introduce our Chablis in a 1.5-liter (51-oz.) bottle and 3-liter (101-oz.) bag.

Sparkling-wine lovers rejoiced in the introduction of Hillebrand's Canadian Champagne. It was produced from a special cuvée of the finest French hybrid and European grape varieties carefully vinified to preserve a fresh, crisp taste. The exceptional quality of this champagne was recognized with a bronze medal at the prestigious Intervin International Competition in 1986. This was the first sparkling wine made in North America to use the low-histamine yeast developed by the Underberg Laboratories in Switzerland.

Peter Mielzynski Jr., Peter Mielzynski Agencies' manager in Alberta, surprised all of us by getting a general listing for Schloss Hillebrand and a special listing for the Gewürztraminer at the Alberta Liquor Control Board. This was the first order of Hillebrand wines outside the province of Ontario.

Nineteen eighty-five was an excellent year for Hillebrand at international wine competitions. That year, at the International Eastern Wine Competition in New York, the 1984 vintage Eiswein was awarded a gold—only the second gold medal ever to be awarded to a Canadian wine at this important show. At the same competition our Étienne Brûlé Blanc won the bronze medal, and our 1984 vintage Vidal received an honorable mention. Earlier in the year, in London, England, at the prestigious International Wine and Spirit Competition, the 1984 Vidal Eiswein captured a silver medal, and the highest score ever awarded to a Canadian wine! These awards resulted in positive press coverage in Canada and internationally for Hillebrand.

Besides winning competitions, we were also selling wine. In 1985, wine sales increased by 52.6 percent over the previous year; Hillebrand sold a total of 62,066 9-liter (304-oz.) cases.

Growth continued into the new year. Early in 1986 we started planning, together with architect Stan Szaflarski, the new 1,182-square-meter (13,130-square-foot) expansion for the winery. In this new facility, we wanted to install a bottling line and stainless-steel storage tanks for the wine that was ready to be bottled. We needed a large storage space for empty bottles and the cases of wine that were ready for shipment. We also required a loading dock to facilitate shipping. At the back of the building, we planned a cellar for ageing the wines in oak barrels. The main company offices were to be located on the second floor and the entrance would be from the mezzanine. The working drawings and tender documents were completed by April 1986. The tenders were called in May, and the project was assigned to Bromac Construction and Engineering Ltd., of Fenwick, Ontario. Construction started immediately, as it was critical for us to complete the project by January 1987.

Next to the new bottling line, we planned to install the equipment needed for the production of the sparkling wines, using the Charmat process (*méthode Charmat*). This method of making sparkling wines is tank-based as opposed to the classic *méthode champenoise*, which involves bottle fermentation. This purchase was approved by the Underberg Company at an estimated cost of $300,000, but a government grant defrayed the amount by $100,000.

Until 1986 the Underberg Company, the majority shareholder of Hillebrand Estates Winery, had not required Joe Pohorly to contribute according to his shares. Now, since the winery was doing well, the Underberg Company made it clear that they expected Joe to carry his

portion of the obligation in the new investments and give the necessary guarantees to the bank for the mortgage on the new building.
Joe decided that he would rather sell his 33.3 percent share to
Underberg and resign as president of Hillebrand. He wished to return
to an engineering career. Emil Underberg recognized Joe's contribution to Hillebrand's success and agreed to purchase Joe's shares,
paying a very fair price for them.

Now we needed to look for a new president. We didn't have to look
far. John Swan, vice president of Hillebrand, had already proved to be
an excellent negotiator and innovator, and he represented Hillebrand
effectively as a member of the Wine Council of Ontario. In 1986, he
was appointed as the new president of Hillebrand Estates Winery.

From John's first day at Hillebrand, his mind had been set on
building a positive working relationship with the grape growers. As
stated earlier, he was convinced that quality wines begin with quality
grapes, planted in proper soil in a suitable micro-climate (see page
54). To get to know the grape growers, he started inviting them, a few
at a time, to early-morning breakfasts at a nearby restaurant, the
Dew Drop, where he shared with them the wine-marketing experiences he had acquired in England. They, in turn, talked about their
expertise. The growers were very interested to learn about the world
wine trends and particularly about the increasing popularity of
Chardonnay. Winemakers worldwide were developing different styles
of Chardonnay, providing consumers with a great selection. John
explained that Sauvignon Blanc and Riesling were also increasing in
popularity. The growers had themselves noticed the range of white
varietal wines sold at LCBO stores.

The LCBO's change to self-service stores had changed customers'
buying habits and had increased their interest in learning about
wines. In many large LCBO stores, wine consultants were available to
help inform prospective customers. Consumers could also learn about
new brands from articles written by wine critics like Tony Aspler, Bob
Pennington, Andrew Sharp and others. Gone were the days when

some people would buy a bottle of cheap domestic sherry when they could not afford a bottle of their favorite rye whisky! Wine was coming of age in Ontario, becoming established in Canadian culture.

As I mentioned earlier, I spent some of my most enjoyable moments selling wines in Hillebrand's stores and getting to talk directly to our customers. One day, right after Christmas, I was working in one of our stores when a middle-aged man brought in a parcel wrapped in Christmas paper. Inside there were three bottles of our wines—Schloss Hillebrand, Le Baron Blanc and Étienne Brûlé Blanc. He asked for a refund, explaining that this was a gift and that he did not drink Ontario wines. I was rather surprised and pointed out to him that it must be difficult to judge a wine without ever tasting it. With a little hesitation he insisted that in his opinion all Canadian wines were undrinkable. I asked him if he would give me an opportunity to explain the changes taking place in the Ontario wine industry. I compared his usual brand, Blue Nun, of German origin, to our Schloss and offered him double the refund if he would try the wines he got at Christmas and still found them not to his taste. He agreed. A few days later I went to see him, and he sheepishly told me that he was delighted with our wines.

There was no doubt that since its inception Hillebrand Winery had sparked the interest of many growers to plant classic varieties of grapes. Varietal wines of quality are created in the vineyards and the cellar, and crafted by the skill and philosophy of the winemaker. John Swan recognized the interdependence between the winery and the grape growers, and as a result, an extremely important decision was made: Hillebrand extended a 10-year contract to the growers. This would oblige the winery to purchase all varieties of quality grapes from them over this period of time. The news was enthusiastically received by the growers. Such a contract would help them secure financing for planting new vines and assure them a market for their crop. This in turn would cement a true partnership between the growers and the winery. Hillebrand's viticulturist and winemaking staff were on hand to offer educational seminars and assistance on improving the quality of grapes.

During 1986, Hillebrand sold more than 8,000 cases of classical varieties of wines through its own stores and LCBO outlets. Because of growing demand for our Chardonnay, Pinot Noir, Riesling, Cabernet Sauvignon, Vidal, Seyval and Maréchal Foch, John Swan decided to purchase double the amount of grapes to assure meeting the future demand. Seven new stores would be in full operation by the end of the year, making a total of 14.

With talk of free trade with the United States in the air, Hillebrand had to be ready for real competition, should the deal between Canada and the United States be finalized. Most of the Californian wines were produced from the French varieties of grapes. Hillebrand was seriously concerned that California would flood the market with its wines. We needed a development strategy, starting off by classifying the wines into categories or, better said, into series.

In the first place, Hillebrand started a program for Chardonnay and Riesling, the two varietals that had the most potential and were timely in the market. It was a known fact that these two grape varieties were successful in the Niagara wine region, and the sales of the Harvest Chardonnay were growing steadily. With the arrival of a new winemaker, subsequent programs would be created for other important varietals, such as Merlot, Cabernet Franc and Cabernet Sauvignon.

After two years of experimenting in viticulture at Hillebrand, and studying horticulture at Guelph University, Greg Berti graduated with a Bachelor of Science degree. Shortly afterward, he was hired as a full-time viticulturist at Hillebrand Estates Winery. (At the time, ours was the only winery employing a full-time viticulturist.) During his hands-on studies at Hillebrand, Greg had learned a great deal from

Andreas Gestaltner about the art of winemaking. And, through his association with the grape growers, he'd discovered how challenging and important the role of a viticulturist had become in the long and exacting process of wine production.

We were in the process of selecting the vineyards with desirable micro-climatic conditions so as to develop single-vineyard Chardonnays. Micro-climate refers to a specific set of climatic features that distinguish one area over another. In a micro-climate, grapes display certain characteristics unique to that area. Aspects such as height of location, incline and number of hours of sunshine, combined with soil composition (gravel, clay, chalk), create a micro-climate that's suitable for specific grape varieties.

There is a strip of land between the Niagara Escarpment and Lake Ontario, 11 kilometers (7 miles) wide and 56 kilometers (35 miles) long, that exhibits several distinct micro-climatic conditions. This area is comparable to the wine regions of Alsace in France, and closely mirrors Burgundy, France, the birthplace of Chardonnay. Knowledge of each micro-climate comes from experimenting with vines and tracking the results over a number of years to find the ideal grape variety that would produce a wine of a certain character. In the Niagara region, for example, we found that a small parcel of vineyard in the area, known as the Bench, below the Niagara Escarpment, produced wines whose character was distinct from those produced in the area at the foothills closer to Lake Ontario. These distinctions gave rise to the single-vineyard concept, which in turn helped to delineate various zones of production in Niagara.

Initially, John Swan approached two excellent vineyards, already working with Hillebrand under the 10-year contract. These were Huebel Estates Vineyards and Seeger Estates Vineyards. Huebel Vineyards was situated between the Niagara Escarpment and Lake Ontario, near Queenston. It was blessed with one of the most favorable climatic locations. The vines were the first to sprout in spring and the first to flower in summer. Moreover, Huebel Vineyards provided ideal harvesting conditions when the grapes were at the perfect moment of maturity. Huebel Estates Vineyards was managed by Matthias Oppenlaender, who immigrated to Ontario from Germany in 1985 to run the vineyard. It had been planted for the first time in the spring of 1984. Ideal micro-climatic conditions at Huebel promised great harvests of Chardonnay, Riesling, Pinot Gris, Sauvignon Blanc, Cabernet Franc and Cabernet Sauvignon. When Matthias was approached by John Swan with the proposal to grow special Chardonnay grapes for the single-vineyard Chardonnay series, he was very interested and promised his full cooperation.

Albrecht Seeger, together with his parents, had been growing premium vinifera grapes in Seeger Estates Vineyards since 1978. They belonged to the Niagara wine region pioneers who had been experimenting and constantly improving the white and red grape varieties. The Seegers had been Hillebrand's suppliers since 1983 and were the first to be offered the 10-year Hillebrand contract. Their acres of prime vine estate had given Hillebrand the assurance for the future supply of the best-quality varietals. Albrecht Seeger was very supportive of Hillebrand's plan to introduce single-vineyard Chardonnays. There was no doubt that he would deliver the best-quality Chardonnay grapes, picked at the moment of optimum maturity.

Growers were beginning to be excited about Hillebrand's advancement in producing quality varietal wines. This provided the confidence and incentive for them to grow world-class grapes.

6

AN ARTISTIC COLLABORATION

ne of the most important events in the history of Hillebrand Estates Winery was the launch, in September 1986, of the first Collectors' Choice series of 1985 vintage Pinot Noir and Chardonnay. Both wines had been specially vinted for the Collectors' Choice series and were complemented by labels featuring two Tom Thomson paintings, *Aura Lee Lake* and *Snow Shadows*. A special, limited number of these collectors' wines had been bottled and individually numbered.

The story behind the Collectors' Choice labels is worth telling.

Back when I worked at McGuinness Distillery, we sought to create labels that would identify our products with Canadian culture. One of the best examples was the packaging we developed for the eight-year-old Old Canada whisky. The label was a replica of the famous painting *Bilking the Toll*, by Cornelius Krieghoff, painted at Longueuil in Quebec in 1861. Old Canada whisky became a popular seller across Canada and was extremely successful in exports to Germany. The label conjured up images of Canada's pioneer history, and it appealed to customers. On a more contemporary note, when the CN Tower was nearing completion, the distillery created CN Tower whisky, in a bottle shaped exactly like the tower itself. The brand was enthusiastically received in the domestic market, where pride in the CN Tower accomplishment was high. It also sold well abroad and became a favorite for tourists wanting a truly Canadian gift for friends and family.

It was my goal to find a similar vehicle for Hillebrand's quality varietal wines. I wanted to find a way of linking Canadian culture to the Niagara wine-growing area. In discussions with Joe Pohorly and John Swan we decided that Canadian paintings would interpret, most beautifully, the association we wanted to create. We resolved to approach the McMichael Foundation to obtain permission to replicate the paintings of Tom Thomson and the Group of Seven on the labels of our highest-quality varietals—the Collectors' Choice series.

The McMichael Canadian Art Gallery has its own interesting history. In 1951 Robert and Signe McMichael purchased 4 hectares (10 acres) of land in the village of Kleinburg, Ontario, and built a cozy pioneer-style home, which they named Tapawingo (a native word meaning "place of joy").

They started collecting paintings by Tom Thomson and the Group of Seven and, as the collection and interest from the public grew, the McMichaels extended the floor area of their house to 929 square meters (10,000 square feet). They also began to investigate ways to make the gallery permanently accessible to the public.

In 1965, following lengthy negotiations with the province of Ontario, the McMichaels transferred ownership of their home, 4 hectares (10 acres) of property and a collection of 194 paintings to the government. In return, the provincial government agreed to ensure that the collection, buildings and grounds would be maintained and that the original spirit of the collection—to collect works by "Tom Thomson, Emily Carr, David Milne, A. Y. Jackson, Lawren Harris, A. J. Casson, Frederick Varley, Arthur Lismer, J. E. H. MacDonald, Franklin Carmichael, who have made contributions to the development of Canadian art." Robert and Signe McMichael had made a most generous contribution to Canadians by donating their home, property and collection to the province of Ontario. The many visitors the gallery attracted were testimony to the pride Canadians have in their artistic heritage.

John Swan presented Hillebrand's proposal to the board of trustees of the McMichael Collection in Kleinburg. Winemaking, he told the board, is an art with a time-honored tradition that is appropriately associated with beautiful paintings. The board members, and Robert McMichael himself, responded positively to our concept. The first step, they advised John, was for him to talk to Ontario's Ministry of Culture. The bicentennial committee members, with whom Hillebrand already had a positive track record, assisted John in making appropriate government contacts. Norman Best, executive director of the bicentennial committee, had visited the Hillebrand winery several times, and was well aware how much money and work had gone into maximizing the quality of our wines. He supported our proposal and made favorable recommendations to the Ministry of Culture.

In 1986, Hillebrand finally received the news that we had been waiting for. We had reason to celebrate! As a result of John Swan's negotiations with the McMichael board of trustees and the Ontario government's Ministry of Culture, Hillebrand Estates Winery was awarded an eight-year exclusive contract to replicate the gallery's paintings on our Collectors' Choice labels.

The introduction of these wines was celebrated with a gala dinner at the McMichael Canadian Art Gallery, under the patronage of Robert and Signe McMichael. Over 100 guests joined the celebration.

By the end of 1986, annual sales had reached 97,128 cases (9 liters [304 oz.] per case). Of this total, 14 Hillebrand stores had sold 43,541 cases (44.8 percent), and 48,513 cases (49.9 percent) were sold through LCBO stores. The special label orders and shipments to the Alberta Liquor Control Board and to Air Canada accounted for 5,074 cases (5.3 percent). Of total sales, 90 percent were our quality generic wines, while 10 percent consisted of varietals. This last category offered the greatest growth potential.

For the next five years, the grape growers were able to supply Hillebrand with larger amounts of Chardonnay, Riesling, Merlot, Cabernet Franc and Cabernet Sauvignon grapes, and Hillebrand Winery was able to develop and market high-quality varietals.

With the completion of the new building, the new barrel-ageing cellar was ready. This facility would be used for ageing some of our best varietals, primarily using French oak barrels, which at $600 each added considerably to the cost of production. The new cellar would support our barrel-aged and barrel-fermented Chardonnay, Cabernet and Merlot programs. It would also augment Hillebrand's tour program.

Hillebrand Winery needed a minimum of 40 retail stores in Ontario to allow for wider distribution, to become better known and to grow its customer base. The winery had to open as many wine stores as possible, before the LCBO stopped issuing retail wine store licenses—a reality we anticipated in the event of a free trade agreement being signed and approved by the Canadian and U.S. governments. The winery already owned 14 stores. To meet our goals, a further 26 stores would have to be opened in the near future. That would require an additional $650,000 investment by the Underberg Company. Emil Underberg and his consultant, Gerd Peskes, understood the urgency of the project and approved the plan. We'd overcome the first hurdle of financing, but we faced many more challenges. To find suitable store locations then hire and train the personnel to meet Hillebrand's standards was a formidable task.

Many new distinctions were awarded to Hillebrand Estates Winery in 1986:

International Eastern Wine Competition (U.S.)

Schloss Hillebrand ∿ *Bronze Medal*
Canadian Champagne, 1985 ∿ *Bronze Medal*
Collectors' Choice Chardonnay, 1985 ∿ *Bronze Medal*
Cabernet Merlot, 1985 ∿ *Quality Wine Award*
Eiswein, 1985 ∿ *Quality Wine Award*

Intervin International Competition (U.S.)

Eiswein, 1985 ∿ *Silver Medal*
Canadian Champagne ∿ *Bronze Medal*

International Wine and Spirit Competition (U.K.)

Eiswein, 1984 ∿ *Bronze Medal*

The year had ended with many great successes for Hillebrand. However, there was a serious problem facing the winery and, for that matter, every business in Canada: Fast-rising interest rates were severely reducing anticipated profits.

At the beginning of January 1987 the administrative offices were ready to be moved to the new expansion building. The Wine Centre was relocated to the former administrative offices. Plans were also under way to renovate the old second-floor offices, at a cost of $170,000. An elegant room with tasting facilities was needed to host the winery's VIP functions. This room was to display the medals and framed certificates won at international competitions. (These renovations were completed in November 1987.)

There was now a large assembly hall from which visitors to the winery proceeded to the video room. Here they watched a presentation about the many operational aspects of the winery, from grape pressing to bottling, and learned about the grape-growing areas of Niagara-on-the-Lake. A tour of the winery followed. The first stop was the 4 hectares (10 acres) behind the winery, which was used as an experimental plot. Greg Berti had planted rows of different varietals and identified each row with a plaque. Visitors could see, firsthand, the varietals from which our wines were produced. After viewing the barrel-ageing cellars at the completion of the tour, the participants returned to the assembly hall, where they could taste and buy the wines of their choice. The Hillebrand winery store had been enlarged, making it fully self-service, with a large wine-tasting counter. The store also carried a range of wine accessories, books about the wine regions of the world and many interesting pamphlets.

The Wine Centre embodied the potential of the winery, and programs were initiated to maximize its use. The well-trained staff met regularly with the winemaker and the viticulturist to share information. Knowing about wine/grape developments and the progress of the company enabled tour staff to enthusiastically project Hillebrand's quality image. The tour staff, in turn, provided the winemaker with feedback from the customers. This provided a direct link to customer preferences that informed his winemaking. The Wine Centre had another very important objective: It was used to educate Hillebrand's retail staff who were then able to inform their customers about the latest wine trends.

A gathering of nearly 200 people was held at Hillebrand Estates Winery on July 23, 1987, to celebrate the formal opening of the Wine Information Centre Building and the new cellars. The Honorable Jim Bradley, MPP for St. Catharines (unofficially dubbed the minister of wine by the industry, for his championing of Niagara wines), officiated at the opening. Also present were Emil Underberg, Jack Ackroyd, chairman of the LCBO, Doug McLennan and John Fawcett of the Royal Bank of Canada, wine critic and writer Andrew Sharp, our grape growers and their families, Hillebrand employees and their families and Peter Mielzynski Agencies' management and representatives.

Jim Bradley congratulated everyone at Hillebrand Estates Winery for providing great leadership and direction to the grape and wine producers of Ontario, bringing recognition of the quality of wines produced, both in Canada and overseas. He remarked that the new Wine Information Centre would attract even more visitors and tourists.

Emil Underberg took the opportunity to thank the management and staff for making Hillebrand Estates Winery such a success. He praised the grape growers for their collaboration with the winery. This cooperation, he said, encouraged him to continue to invest in the equipment and the best-qualified personnel. Emil emphasized that he was well aware of many growers who had invested a great deal of money by discarding the North American varieties of grapes and replacing them with the classical varieties. He acknowledged that a key factor in Hillebrand's success was the absolute reliance on excellent-quality grapes. Emil concluded his comments by offering, as an incentive, a two-week trip to the grape-growing areas of Germany for the best grape producer and guest.

Following Emil Underberg's speech, John Swan announced that a new press house was to be built. In addition to the Europress, the winery had purchased a Bucher Press, which would be needed to handle the greatly increased volume of grapes from the 1988 harvest. Furthermore, he told the group, a dripping tank system for the production of the white wines would be installed. John explained how the system worked: "Grapes are handpicked from single vineyards and carefully placed in the specially designed tall steel hopper tank. The weight of the grapes causes the grape skins to burst naturally and the juice runs freely into a trough at the bottom of the tank, which then takes the juice to a small stainless-steel fermentation tank. By this 'gentle persuasion,' and by avoiding pressing or crushing the skins, the juice retains the fruit character, making for a wine with true varietal character." (This system of using only the free-run juice would be introduced for the first time for both the Single Vineyard Chardonnay and Collectors' Choice Chardonnay.)

John added that the Vinimatic Tank, for the production of red wines, would be used for the first time in Canada at Hillebrand Estates Winery. The Vinimatic was considered the Mercedes-Benz for juice extraction. He explained that since red wine is the product of skin and juice, the Vinimatic's role is to ensure constant contact between them. In a traditional fermentation tank skins float to the top. The pump at the bottom of the tank pumps constantly, circulating the juice, stirring in the skins and allowing oxygen to reach the must. With the Vinimatic, fins stir the skin and juice while the tank turns. This, together with the controlled heating of the tank during fermentation, allows a maximum extraction of flavor and skin pigmentation. John indicated that the new press house would provide another step for Hillebrand toward producing the best-quality wines in Canada.

Emil Underberg's comments and John Swan's announcements had a profound impact on the gathering—especially on our grape growers. The growers clearly heard that they were much more than suppliers. They had been publicly acknowledged as full participants in the winemaking process. The celebrations ended with a festive lunch, complemented by the choicest wines of the Hillebrand Winery.

FREE TRADE AND
THE WINE INDUSTRY

*I*n the mid-1980s, discussions were under way that would permanently affect the future of the Canadian wine industry. In
March 1985 U.S. president Ronald Reagan visited Canada for
the Free Trade Summit Meeting with Prime Minister Brian Mulroney.
The meeting took place in historic Quebec City. At the conclusion of
the summit both Reagan and Mulroney and their wives sung *When
Irish Eyes Are Smiling*. The message was distinctly upbeat.

Soon after these talks the principles of a North American Free Trade
Agreement (NAFTA) were widely discussed and debated by the federal
and provincial governments. There was much controversy. The premiers of Ontario, Manitoba and Prince Edward Island opposed NAFTA,
while the premiers of Quebec, Nova Scotia and Newfoundland endorsed
it. The other provinces were undecided. Only a small part of the agreement, involving less than 10 percent of the trade between the two countries, required provincial cooperation. Prime Minister Mulroney, with
his Conservative government, decided to continue NAFTA negotiations
with the United States. He formed a very strong Canadian team headed
by Simon Reisman, former deputy minister of finance. The very complex
negotiations went on throughout 1986, with slow progress.

Traditional basket press used in 1983 for outdoor pressing of Hillebrand's
Vidal Eiswein grapes.

Hillebrand 1983 vintage Eiswein was the first domestically produced Eiswein in Ontario sold through the Liquor Control Board of Ontario.

The Hillebrand wines Étienne Brûlé Rouge and Étienne Brûlé Blanc were declared the official wines for the Ontario Bicentennial celebrations in 1984.

John Swan (right), president of Hillebrand Estates Winery, welcomes Robert Mielzynski, newly graduated from Fresno State University with a Bachelor of Science in oenology and viticulture.

The Bucher Grape Press, an example of how Hillebrand invested in state-of-the-art winemaking equipment.

The Collectors' Choice limited edition wines, bearing labels of the Group of Seven paintings.

Mounier, sparkling wine made in the traditional *méthode champenoise*.

The Trius series became the "flagship" of Hillebrand and was designed to perfectly embody the trio of steps in wine production: the cultivating and harvesting of the grapes, the winemaking and the marketing.

Canadian wine producers knew that they could be seriously affected if the free trade negotiations led to a signed agreement between the United States and Canada. There were competitive factors working against our wine producers. First, increased competition from the American wineries with their increased distribution and lower markups at the liquor boards threatened Canadian profits. Another key factor was that the Liquor License Board of Ontario (LLBO) would no longer issue retail wine store licenses to domestic wineries. It was thought that this would disadvantage our trading partners because imported wines have to be sold through the government stores.

As a member of the Ontario Wine Council, John Swan had solid connections with the Ontario government and was very well aware of the potential problems the wine industry faced. He also knew the concerns of the grape growers, whose relationship to the winery had become one of close cooperation. By early 1987 free trade negotiations started to show progress. An agreement seemed to be right around the corner.

At Hillebrand we faced a time crunch. The two additional stores, which were crucial for the realization of the winery's expansion goals, needed to be opened sooner than we had anticipated. The original plan had called for the stores to be opened during the next four years. But once NAFTA was signed, we would find ourselves with little time before the LLBO would have to stop issuing permits for new stores. Opening additional stores presented another challenge. We would also have to increase production. Current supply would not meet future demand.

John Swan and Greg Berti met with our grape growers to discuss supply needs. Hillebrand had to substantially increase the volume of grapes purchased for the 1987 vintage. And in subsequent years even more grapes would be needed. Fourteen 60,000-liter-capacity (15,850-gal.) fermentation tanks had been installed in the newly built cellar, equipped with powerful air conditioners to assure the low temperatures required for slow fermentation of the white wines.

More storage tanks were built outside to stabilize the wine from tartrates, a white colorless crystalline present in grape juice and deposited during fermentation of wines, throughout the cold winter months. This is the usual solution in our cold Canadian climate.

The Underberg Company came up with the funds to invest in all the projects, and John Swan made the decision to open 14 new stores in 1987 and an additional 16 in 1988. It was not easy to find suitable locations in such a short time and to simultaneously hire and train new staff. John's focus was to find the right locations. He knew exactly what he was looking for. The manager of the College Park store, David Gibson, was chosen to supervise the building of the stores to our specifications. His mandate was to design stores that would convey a welcoming atmosphere to customers. A new department was created and a new manager hired who would be responsible for the operations and profitability of Hillebrand's stores.

With store expansion under way we turned our attention to helping our customers make informed purchases. Since our new bottling line could handle both front and back labels, we decided to create back labels (see Appendix 1), which would inform our customers, in detail, about the content and quality of our products. The back labels were used on all our wines. This met with our customers' instant approval. Feedback from Peter Mielzynski Agencies' representatives indicated that the informative back labels were also greatly appreciated by the staff at LCBO stores and by restaurant wine buyers. We also developed pamphlets using the information from the back labels. These were available in every Hillebrand store and to visitors touring the winery.

In October 1987, the North America Free Trade Agreement was finalized. In order for NAFTA to be in force by the scheduled date of January 1, 1989, the legislation had to be passed swiftly by the Canadian houses of parliament and the U.S. Congress. At first it looked like plain sailing. The bill was approved by a clear majority of members of parliament. Indeed, on second reading it was ratified by

114 votes to 51. However, the Liberal majority in the Senate would not approve NAFTA. Prime Minister Brian Mulroney was forced to call a general election in September 1988 for November 1988. Free trade was the main campaign issue for all parties.

John Swan wrote his own perspective on NAFTA. It appeared in the *Toronto Star* on November 13, 1987, eight days before the election. Because his message is so important to the story of Hillebrand, I quote it here in full.

AN ONTARIO WINERY THAT WELCOMES FREE TRADE

In light of all the negative views on free trade that have been reflected by many in the wine industry, I would like to express to the public and my wine industry colleagues why Hillebrand Estates Winery is optimistic about the deal.

All the nervousness in the wine industry over free trade and the media predictions of doom are just initial reactions to something no one completely understands. I experienced a similar situation when I worked in England for a well-known European wine company during the time when Britain was negotiating to enter the European Economic Community Trade Agreement. A similar hysteria broke out there when British wine distributors became concerned about the effect it [the agreement] would have on them. What the trade agreement did for the British industry as a whole was to make it more streamlined and in the long term more efficient. This is exactly what I expect to happen here.

Yes, some wineries will close down, but those committed to producing world-class wines will challenge the competition. Canadian wineries are now producing international award-winning wines from the grapes grown in Niagara, where climatic conditions are ideal for growing world-class premium grapes. Hillebrand wouldn't be tying up ten-year contracts now, with the local grape growers, if we weren't planning to continue purchasing from those farmers who are providing us with these grapes. For varietal (European hybrid) grapes, the costs are very competitive with prices from U.S. farmers and likewise, Canadian premium varietal wines are competitive and will remain so.

The key word here is premium. The market for premium wines is and will remain totally separate from the market for jug wines. Hillebrand will not compete in the jug wine market.

The big boys in Canada have been forced to open up secondary divisions in other provinces to avoid paying the high tariffs being placed on wines traded between the provinces. If inter-provincial tariffs are dropped as part of the free trade deal, or to conform with this week's ruling of the General Agreement on Tariffs and Trade, you will see these secondary plants fazed [sic] out. But you'll also see expansion at the home base and much more efficiency in the long run. Operating costs will be drastically reduced and prices will reflect that, thus making them more competitive with California's so-called big boys. It will take a strong political will from federal and provincial governments to remove the inter-provincial liquor board tariffs. We must receive national treatment, east to west as well as north and south.

When I came to Hillebrand in February, 1984, we knew free trade was on the horizon. Experience told me that establishing a niche for Hillebrand in the marketplace would be at the top of my priority list. Our niche is our European-style wine market stores, which directly service our clients. We have opened twenty-six such stores across Southern Ontario in the past three years and our store network is continuing to grow at a rapid pace.

Educating the public about Hillebrand and the Canadian wine industry as a whole is our primary objective. To become recognised as a world-class wine producing region as well respected as Bordeaux and Burgundy is the direction Hillebrand is pursuing, and we hope our fellow wineries will also focus on this objective. The recent proposal made for funding, to create a wine route through the Niagara region, is evidence that we are one step closer to that. A wine education centre has been added to our facilities, and our wine tasting tours are now operating year round. At the point of purchase, our wine merchants in the retail stores have been extensively trained to offer knowledgeable professional advice. We are so confident in our product and our sales staff that as soon as the LCBO approves it, we will offer a selection of premium wines from the U.S. in our stores. Those wines which have achieved standards of excellence equal to our own will sit side by side with Hillebrand Estates' wines.

We have become the largest producer of varietal wines in Ontario. Our long-term sales goal is relatively small in comparison to that of the major wineries, but we feel that, in order to control superior quality in our wines, it is important to limit production. Our size will remain that of an estate winery as it always has been intended.

I believe as Canadians continue to see Hillebrand and other Canadian wineries taking prestigious awards in international competitions, and as they start to see them compete successfully with some of the world's most well-known wines, a feeling of patriotism toward wine and all Canadian products will emerge.

John Swan's article made a significant impression on its readers. The day following its release, CBC-TV interviewed John on how free trade might affect the wine industry in Canada. Our store managers reported how much our customers appreciated the realistic outlook on free trade that John had expressed in his article.

John's positive outlook did not go unnoticed by the federal government, as witnessed in a letter of thanks from then external affairs minister John Crosbie.

At around the same time the elections were taking place, Benoit (Ben) Huchin, an experienced French winemaker, was hired by John Swan. He was to replace Andreas Gestaltner in July of the following year. Andreas, who had to return home, had agreed to stay and help Ben with the 1987 harvest. It promised to be very busy because Hillebrand had purchased double the amount of grapes over the previous year. Both winemakers would be assisted by the viticulturist Greg Berti, who had worked for Hillebrand since the beginning of the year. Greg would be a great help to the winemakers in finding the required quality grapes for making different series of Chardonnays and Rieslings.

At the same time that Ben was hired at Hillebrand, my son Robert graduated from Fresno State University, California, with a Bachelor of Science degree in oenology and viticulture. Robert was already the proud owner of 5 percent of Hillebrand Estates Winery shares, which, in part, he had acquired as a gift from Emil Underberg and me. Robert had lived with the Underberg family at Haus Balken in West Germany throughout his high school years. He had attended the American International School in Düsseldorf and had shared his life with Emil and Tina's children.

There is no doubt that Robert's stay at Haus Balken was both pleasant and educational. Tina Underberg insisted that her children and Robert help to entertain guests, set the table for dinners, choose the right flowers for decoration, offer the appropriate wine glasses and, with Emil's guidance, select the appropriate wines. Emil Underberg had a modern and temperature-controlled wine cellar, where he collected the best vintages of the most famous château wines from France. He particularly enjoyed the Mosel wines. The brands, which his company represented in many European countries, were visibly displayed in a small room next to the wine cellar. Martel cognacs, Metaxa brandies, Haig & Haig whiskies, Bacardi rum, Jack Daniel's Tennessee Whisky, as well as the famous Polish Vodka Wyborowa were among his clients.

Emil liked to smoke a good cigar with his friends after dinner. He had a special temperature-controlled vault built where he kept his best cigars, purchased from Davidoff Store in London, England. And Underberg Natural Herb Bitters were made available in every room, set in specially designed crystal holders, accompanied by the most attractive and very unusual tall glasses. Emil and Tina were very meticulous, yet uncommonly creative, whether at home or at the office.

Emil Underberg often hired consultants, usually with technical expertise, to help improve the quality of the brands his company was producing. Perhaps the best known of these was Underberg Digestive, the remedy that became famous for its digestive characteristics. Underberg Research Laboratories, located in Zurich, was the center where professors and technicians worked to discover new methods of producing foods free of histamines (good news for people suffering from allergies). All these concepts and new ideas were always discussed with the children at home, and Emil and Tina liked to hear their ideas and even their constructive criticism.

Robert took part in these discussions and was greatly influenced by the positive atmosphere of the Underberg home. During his summer holidays he worked in many different wineries in Europe. Then, as planned, he went to further his interest in wine by studying oenology at Fresno State University. In order to gain experience in wine selling and marketing, Robert used his vacation time to work for a small exclusive California wine distributor, Central Coast Wine Company. This gave him the opportunity to participate in strategic marketing meetings at a number of wine estates that were represented by Central Coast.

After graduation, Emil Underberg offered Robert the position of vice president at Hillebrand Estates Winery. Before accepting such a responsible position, Robert felt that he should have more practical experience with different, traditional, well-known wine estates in Europe. Emil agreed to Robert's plan to spend an additional 12 months in Europe.

By 1987, in addition to Château des Charmes Estates Winery and Inniskillin Winery, Hillebrand Estates Winery was facing competition from six new estate wineries—Cave Spring Cellars, Vineland Estates

Winery, Reif Estate Winery, Henry of Pelham Winery, Konzelmann Estate Winery and Stoney Ridge Cellars. All these new wineries were growing the classic varietal grapes of excellent quality, and some would sell their excess crop to other wineries. From the very beginning, one of Hillebrand's best suppliers of grapes was Ewald Reif, whose family began winemaking in Germany's Rhine region in the nineteenth century. Immigrating to Canada in 1977, the Reifs chose the Niagara-on-the-Lake area to carry on their family's tradition.

Ewald Reif and his brother found the best possible area for their future vineyards only minutes from Niagara-on-the-Lake and steps away from the banks of the Niagara River. Following five years of intensive work, the vineyard's potential became evident. The finest European vinifera vines produced grapes that initially helped the Inniskillin Winery in its production of fine wines. Later, Hillebrand became the beneficiary of Reif's superb grapes. In 1983, Ewald Reif's nephew, Klaus, a recent graduate of the world-famous University of Geisenheim near Frankfurt, Germany, opened the doors of Reif Estates Winery to the public. From the very beginning Klaus worked closely with his uncle, who, through years of hard work, had become one of Niagara's most successful growers of classic varietals.

There was no doubt that the wines produced by the Ontario estate wineries helped to create a better image for the Niagara wine region. Thousands of visitors, who initially came to see Niagara Falls, now included the wineries on their itinerary. They made their rounds of the wineries, and enjoyed the well-organized, informative tours and wine tastings. The tours won new converts to Ontario wines.

By the end of 1987, Hillebrand Estates Winery owned 26 stores with well-trained and educated staff, whose mission was to inform visitors about our products and to both sell our wines and promote the Niagara wine region. At the beginning of 1987, we had predicted that our stores would outsell the LCBO's sales of our brands. By the end of that year, the total Hillebrand wine sales in Ontario had reached 130,411 cases (in 9-liter [304-oz.] cases), as compared to the

1986 figure of 97,128 cases. Our forecast was correct. Our stores had sold 71,284 cases as compared to the LCBO's total of 59,127 cases.

The success of the stores convinced the Underberg Company to invest in opening a further 16 stores in 1988. This was a timely decision in view of the direction of the free trade talks and their implications for the Ontario market. The federal government had promised the U.S. government a level playing field by reducing the markup levied on American wines. As far as the Ontario wineries were concerned, this meant serious competition in the government-controlled stores since many U.S. wineries had lower overheads and could introduce wines at a lower base price than their Canadian counterparts.

For the Niagara wineries with their own stores there was a window of opportunity. To allow wineries time to adjust to NAFTA, a period of 10 years was allotted, during which wines made from 100 percent Canadian-grown grapes were given a preferential markup. This infuriated the larger domestic wineries, with their dependency on inexpensive imported juice. Hillebrand, with its insistence on quality Canadian grapes and its contracts with Niagara growers, was ready to take advantage of this opportunity. The additional stores would provide the necessary channels to sell the wines with significant profits.

In 1987 Helmuth van Schellenbeck, a director of Underberg Company, spent two months in Canada in order to develop a better understanding of the Canadian market and our wine stores. As I continued to sell wine in our stores one day a week, I asked Helmuth to share in my sales experience. It could have been a bitter pill to swallow for a European executive to become a store clerk, even for a short time, but Helmuth, who had never been on the front line of retail, found the new experience very educational and a lot of fun. Often we had a friendly contest as to who could sell the most bottles!

During his time in Canada, Helmuth became familiar with the complicated system of dealing with the LCBO and the extent to which the wine industry depended on provincial and federal politics. He left with an understanding of how essential it was for Hillebrand to prepare for the unavoidable changes in the wine industry. Helmuth was most impressed with our professionally organized wine tours and the number of people visiting Hillebrand. He learned a great deal during his stay in Canada, and conveyed his appreciation and knowledge of the Ontario wine industry in his subsequent discussions with Emil Underberg at their board meetings in Switzerland.

Another person who visited Hillebrand at the time was Gerd Peskes, business consultant to Emil Underberg, whom I had met on a visit to Haus Balken. As a consultant to many large companies in Germany, his troubleshooting skills enabled him to help his clients resolve their financial problems. Emil Underberg solicited his advice mainly with regard to his companies' future strategies. Consequently, Gerd paid a short visit to Hillebrand at least once a year. He very quickly grasped the dynamics of running a wine company, and was able to give us wise and practical advice. He fully understood the need to prepare Hillebrand for the changes in the wine industry that would result from free trade. Gerd fully supported our drive to open as many stores as possible.

Another award-winning year for Hillebrand Estates Winery was 1987. Here are a few of the highlights:

International Eastern Wine Competition (U.S.)

Eiswein, 1985 ~ *Silver Medal*
Cabernet Merlot, 1985 ~ *Bronze Medal*
Schloss Hillebrand ~ *Bronze Medal*
Hillebrand Canadian Champagne ~ *Quality Wine Award*

Intervin International Competition (U.S.)

Canadian Champagne ~ *Silver Medal*
Cabernet Merlot, 1985 ~ *Bronze Medal*

International Wine and Spirit Competition (U.K.)

Riesling, 1985 ∿ *Bronze Medal*
Canadian Champagne ∿ *Bronze Medal*

In September 1987, Hillebrand launched the second Collectors' Choice series. Eight thousand bottles each of Collectors' Choice Chardonnay and Cabernet Merlot were produced that year and labeled with J. E. H. MacDonald's paintings. *Forest Wilderness* was featured on the Chardonnay label and *Algoma Waterfall* on the Cabernet Merlot.

"Canadian wineries often were being accused of trying to look like French or German wineries with similar labels, so we were after truly Canadian-looking labels," said John Swan at a press conference in 1987, "since wine and art go hand in hand, we teamed Canada's best of both and came up with Collectors' Choice."

At the same time as the second series of Collectors' Choice was introduced to the Ontario market, we decided that it would be the ideal time to launch our newly developed Late Harvest Vidal. Offered in a 375-mL.-size (13-oz.) bottle, this completed the trio of our wines made from Vidal grapes. The first had been Hillebrand's Eiswein, then came Étienne Brûlé developed especially for the Ontario bicentennial celebration, and finally the Late Harvest Vidal. Vidal grapes, when left on the vine for an extra four to eight weeks, contribute unique flavors to a wine. The resulting wine, if barrel aged, tends to develop intense, rich and sweet floral aromas with nuances of orange peel, apricots and honey. Late Harvest Vidal is close in taste to Eiswein, but much lighter and less sweet, with usually 11 to 12 percent alcohol. Late Harvest wine can either be served as a chilled aperitif to complement pâté or as a classic dessert wine.

Producing Late Harvest Vidal is a rather expensive process, as the wine has to be made from grapes harvested as late as October or November. It can be compared in style to the French Sauterne wines or to the famous German Auslese. Since the Hillebrand Eiswein was increasing in popularity, winning gold and silver medals, we were confident that the new Late Harvest Vidal would also gain many new customers for Hillebrand Estates Winery.

When the initial plan for Hillebrand was prepared in January 1983, we did not know that five years later the Canadian wine industry would be facing a free trade agreement with the United States that could seriously affect Canadian wine producers and grape growers. At the same time, interest rates had risen to 13 percent, which made Underberg's investments in Hillebrand much more costly than anticipated. Despite these uncertainties, estate wineries in Ontario had gained prestige through the introduction of so many improvements in the style and quality of their wines.

Large Ontario wineries and the Labrusca grape growers and suppliers felt uneasy about what lay ahead, but Hillebrand Estates Winery was not afraid of the free trade challenge. Our company had always maintained that NAFTA would ensure that the Canadian wine industry would become more efficient and competitive. As a result, the consumer would benefit. We maintained our vision to prepare our wines to compete in the world market by producing top-quality wines and by being innovative in marketing these wines. Would we survive NAFTA? Time would tell.

8

WINDS OF CHANGE

*T*he mutual understanding and trust between Hillebrand Estates Winery and its growers is the reason that Hillebrand had become, by 1988, the largest producer of varietal wines in Ontario. The winery had also gained the respect of the industry and become a leader in the premium-wine market.

This did not go unnoticed by the federal government. At the end of 1988, Hillebrand Estates Winery's president, John Swan, attended a dinner in Ottawa honoring the winners of the 1988 Canada Awards for Business Excellence. The awards recognized the ability of Canadian businesses of all sizes and in all sectors of the economy to achieve excellence within a context of international competitiveness. Hillebrand won a Certificate of Merit in the marketing section. The award was presented by the Honorable Robert de Cotret, minister of regional industrial expansion and minister of state for science and technology. Guy Lorriman, manager of the Canada Awards for Business Excellence, said that they received a record-breaking number of entries that year. Hillebrand had won the Certificate of Merit in the face of stiff competition. Hillebrand Estate Winery was the first Canadian wine company to receive a business excellence award.

The award was reported in most major newspapers. This positive press helped to change many peoples' attitudes toward Ontario wines. At Hillebrand we acknowledged that the prestige of the award had to be shared with the Niagara Peninsula's grape growers, whose diligent efforts and determination made our success possible. They had pushed themselves to produce the vinifera white and red varieties, as well as the European hybrids, that were to become the backbone of the Niagara wine industry in the years to come.

With a reliable local source of varietal grapes, plans had already been made in 1987 by John Swan, our winemaker, Ben Huchin, and our viticulturist, Greg Berti, to develop the Single Vineyard Chardonnay, Harvest Chardonnay, Harvest Riesling and Riesling Classic Dry. In order to develop new concepts for these varietal wines, it was most important to have the equipment to separate the quality and style of the specific vineyards, specific areas and different qualities of juice.

This was the main reason that a new press house was built. No expense was spared to install the best equipment. In the grape-receiving area a new de-stemmer was installed to separate the stems from the grapes. Grapes would then pass to drip tanks and to a rototank (Vinimatic), for what is termed "de-juicing." The natural weight of the grapes themselves provides a 60 percent recovery of the highest-quality free-run juice. After several hours of de-juicing, the Europress and the newly purchased Bucher Press performed the task of gently pressing the grapes for additional quality juice extraction. Both presses were computerized, allowing the exact pressure to be maintained for the type of grape being pressed. Once the juice was pressed through the drip tanks, rototank and presses, it was finally clarified through a centrifuge. From here, the juice was pumped through pipes into the fermenting vats.

There were more than 100 stainless-steel fermenting vats at Hillebrand Winery, ranging in size from 500 to 20,000 liters (130 to 5,200 gal.). This enabled the winery to ferment each varietal separately, and also to separate the grapes from different vineyards and locations in the Niagara Peninsula. Every vineyard site has distinct soils, sunlight and trellising systems, which gives a particular grape variety specific characteristics. The separation of grapes from different vineyards during fermentation was to be the key to Hillebrand's quality Riesling and Chardonnay programs.

To put this in context one might look to the wine region of Burgundy in France. Although the winemakers of this region have only two main varietals, Pinot Noir and Chardonnay, the most obvious distinctions have always been the "terroir"—the French term for the wine-growing environment: soil, site, and local climate, and the attributes each of these give to each wine. To allow these differences to express themselves, the winemakers of Burgundy have followed the appellation system, which designates viticultural, or grape-growing, areas of origin as well as certain standards of quality. At its best, it differentiates between both quality levels and differences of character. The latter is usually seen as a combination of the terroir and the skills of the winemaker. A single producer of 10,000 cases of wine is often required to make 20 different wines, corresponding to that many different parcels of land that he or she may own in different appellations.

To respect these differences the wines have to be made separately. This requires a selection of vats of varying sizes. This procedure is also ideal for blending, when one is creating a wine from a number of plots that offer different characteristics to the wine. The wine from plot A might be soft and supple, that from plot B may give a more pronounced acidity and mineral component to the wine. The two together create a whole that is often superior to the individual component parts.

The ability to express such differences was the reason behind the press house at Hillebrand. Our winemaker, Ben Huchin, described the press house as "the most wonderful tool to enhance the winemaking art," but he also knew that to create outstanding varietal wines, he would need quality grapes. Our viticulturist, Greg Berti, was the expert here. Greg, who had worked for many years with the growers of the Niagara region, recognized that even within this relatively small area there are different micro-climates. Each micro-climate has its own unique characteristics, which allows grapes to develop differently in each location. Greg found out that a Chardonnay grown in one micro-climate had marked differences from Chardonnay grapes grown in another. Specifically, these differences related to the acidity, sugar levels and varietal characteristics. Both Ben and Greg, working together, wanted to take full advantage of the new press house to develop the Single Vineyard Chardonnay. This kind of discovery brings with it a creative excitement. One can imagine that the first monk who experimented with Chardonnay in medieval France had a similar sense of accomplishment!

In mid-March 1988, my son Robert arrived in Niagara-on-the-Lake to start his work with Hillebrand Estates Winery. His Bachelor of Science in oenology and viticulture in hand, Robert was returning after almost a year of practical experience in Europe. He'd been involved in the winemaking processes at the famous Château Kirwan in the Margaux region of Bordeaux in France, during the very rainy 1987 vintage. He'd also spent two months at Cordier House, the well-known wine-producing company in Bordeaux, observing their methods of production and sales. Robert then spent several months at the Underberg Research Center in Zurich. He found his work there to be extremely interesting and educational, and learned about the negative effects of poor winemaking on the chemical structure of the finished wine products. One of the research center's most important research topics was the negative effects of histamines in wines. This area of study was designed to assist consumers with serious allergy problems.

To finish his European immersion, Robert had worked in Vienna at the Underberg-owned Schlumberger Winery. For three months he worked under the guidance of Heinz Turk, Schlumberger's master winemaker. Robert was exposed to the production of *méthode Schlumberger* wines (same as the French *méthode champenoise*), the famous sparkling wines of Austria. His hands-on work experiences expanded to include cellar operations and specific techniques for blending still wines used in the production of *méthode Schlumberger* sparkling wines. Schlumberger Winery worked closely with the Underberg Research Center in Zurich and produced sparkling wines that were virtually histamine-free.

When Robert came back to Canada and joined Hillebrand, he was full of enthusiasm, bringing with him extensive knowledge and experience obtained on two continents in the previous 10 years. It did not take long for him to appreciate the fine team working at Hillebrand. He admired the qualities of Hillebrand's master winemaker, Ben Huchin, and the company's viticulturist, Greg Berti. Robert became an excellent addition to that great team.

To grow the market for Hillebrand wines we began to explore export possibilities. In May 1988 an opportunity presented itself in the form of the first wine and spirit exhibition to be held in Tokyo. The Canadian government agreed to sponsor a trade mission and chose Hillebrand Estates Winery and Labatts Brewery as participants. It was a great honor for Hillebrand to represent Canada. John Swan and Glen Hunt, John's assistant, traveled to Tokyo well in advance of the event, ready with many cases of wine samples for display and tasting purposes. The Canadian Chamber of Commerce donated beautiful posters to decorate the stand, thus enhancing our display with images of life in Canada.

The most important and promising wine for export to Japan was our Eiswein. It was very well received and drew the attention of representatives from the Mitsui Company. Company executives subsequently invited John and Glen to a meeting and tastings at their offices. This enormous company had many different divisions, one being a chain of food stores that had the potential to carry our wines. The management at Mitsui was most impressed with our wines. Their preference was for sweeter wines, such as Schloss Hillebrand, Lady Ann, Johannisberg Riesling and Eiswein. Mitsui Company advised John that they would send two members from their quality control department to visit Hillebrand and make a final decision as to which of our wines would most appeal to Japanese customers.

John and Glen were very happy with the outcome of these meetings and the export possibilities. Not only had we received excellent reviews in the Tokyo press, but also Canadian newspapers told the story of the winery's success in introducing Ontario wines to the Japanese market.

The order from Mitsui Company, when it finally came, resulted in the first shipment of Canadian wines to Japan! Our winery had opened the doors for Canadian wines in Japan. Hillebrand's participation in that exhibition had paid off.

As mentioned earlier, according to the terms of the free trade agreement, the LLBO would cease to issue permits for new stores. Winery stores already open, however, would be allowed to operate, as a result of a grandfather clause that exempted them from the new agreement.

By the end of 1987, Hillebrand Estates Winery owned 26 wine stores in Ontario. Over the years Joe Pohorly and Peter Gamble, later John Swan and Greg Berti, had urged the grape growers to plant the classic grape varieties needed for Hillebrand's future winemaking program. As a result, many growers had reduced and eventually eliminated from their vineyard such varieties as de Chaunac, Duchess and Villard Noir. They replaced them with Chardonnay, Riesling, Pinot Noir, Cabernet Merlot and Gamay. Signs saying "Grapes grown exclusively for Hillebrand Estate Winery" were placed in front of the vineyards. Hillebrand's growers were among the few who were posi-tive about the effects of NAFTA.

The confidence among our grape growers increased when they heard the news that Hillebrand Winery had purchased 16 licenses from Barnes Winery. This represented 12 stores already in operation and four permits to build new stores. The licenses for yet more stores had to be negotiated in 1989. They were becoming more and more difficult to obtain, as many large Ontario wineries were applying, and the Liquor License Board was swamped with applications. By 1990 no more licenses were forthcoming.

In 1987 Hillebrand had purchased 1,525 metric tons (1,677 tons) of grapes from the growers. Unfortunately, it was still difficult to buy sufficient quantities of varietal grapes in the Niagara region to satisfy the growing demand. Again, with the rapid increases of the number of our stores, Chardonnay was out of stock for several months.

Ben Huchin and Greg Berti had the very tricky task of determining the quantity of grapes that would be needed for the 1988 vintage. They had to take into consideration future sales at the 16 new stores, vintage programs for our varietal wines during the coming years and the steadily increasing popularity of Hillebrand's Chardonnay. The winery needed a bumper crop, and Greg followed the weather very closely day by day. The winter of 1987–88 was, on average, milder than normal. The spring was cool and dry with bud break occurring a little later than in previous years. The dryness of the spring carried on until July, with the vineyards receiving only half the normal amount of precipitation. These conditions caused great stress to the vineyards. Then the rain came in late July.

Greg forecasted that the size of the French hybrids crop might be 30 percent less than originally anticipated due to the summer's long dry spell. He felt that the varietals would be of exceptional quality, mainly Chardonnay, Cabernet Sauvignon, Merlot and Riesling. Hillebrand needed to purchase 2,900 metric tons (3,190 tons) of grapes (90 percent more than had been purchased in 1987). Greg trusted that, as a result of the growers' ongoing program to plant more premium vinifera and hybrid grapes, by 1990 Hillebrand would have enough grapes to meet its needs.

Hillebrand and other quality-minded estate wineries in Niagara perceived the need for a clear method of distinguishing the best wines for the consumer. With this in mind the Vintners Quality Alliance (VQA) was formed in 1988. Its goal was to allow consumers to witness the growth of serious wineries that were willing to be judged by an official panel of their peers. John Swan saw the significance of these developments and was an active participant in the plans to form the alliance. In the following passage, he expresses how these ideas developed and what they meant at the time:

THE BIRTH OF THE VINTNERS QUALITY ALLIANCE

In the 1980s, winemaking in Ontario was influenced by the European influx of winemakers working in their small estate wineries. They brought with them the experience of working with varietal grapes that are drier in style than the sweet Canadian grapes being grown. These wineries were prepared to invest in experimenting in the vineyards, and in the vinification of their wines, to provide the wines the consumers were beginning to enjoy. The younger generations had become exposed to wines from around the world, through traveling both for business and on holiday. This meant that the wineries selling varietal wines were able to capitalize on this new trend.

The older and normally larger wineries were slow to realize the changes that were taking place. Unfortunately, the attitude of these wineries in their winemaking techniques and marketing strategies provided a poor image for Ontario wines, and imported wines began to take a larger share of the market. Wineries such as Inniskillin and Château des Charmes had worked hard in their attempt to secure changes in the Wine Content Regulations to ensure that consumers understood the types of wine they were drinking. Many of the larger Ontario wineries used European generic names on their labels, leading buyers to believe that they were drinking a wine of high quality from European grape varieties. Naturally, these wineries resisted any changes to improve the quality of their wines as they would need to invest large sums in their winemaking operations and in the vineyards, replanting with vinifera varieties. They had been protected for years by the various Ontario governments that had supported their operations through subsidies and, significantly, by ensuring that their products were predominant in LCBO stores.

By the mid-1980s, an increasing number of estate wineries had opened, including Cave Spring, Konzelmann, Reif and Hillebrand. This provided more support in the push for clearer labeling to the consumer to indicate the type of wine contained in the bottle. Regular meetings were held by the group of estate wineries to persuade the owners of the larger wineries to adopt a self-policing set of regulations for implementing quality standards of wines produced in Ontario. Similar standards are set in other leading wine-producing countries, for example, A.O.C. (Appelation d'Origine Côntrolée), France, D.O.C. (Denominacione di Origine Controllata), Italy, etc.

Frustrated with the lack of progress in reaching an accord within the industry, the estate wineries lobbied the government of Ontario and the Grape Marketing Board to look seriously at their proposals. Moreover, individual estate owners and their winemakers were expressing their concerns to wine writers. The major issue was that public perception of the quality wines they produced was undermined by the poor image of the mass-produced wines being bottled by the larger wineries.

Pressure was mounting in 1987 due to the free trade talks and the apparent threat to the local wine industry, mainly from competition from wineries in the United States, in particular from California.

The "group of five" estate wineries (Hillebrand, Inniskillin, Château des Charmes, Cave Spring and Reif) decided to urgently formulate self-governing rules, to provide clear recognition to wines in Ontario produced from locally grown world-class grapes. The symbol VQA (Vintners Quality Alliance) was decided upon, and an insignia was designed. This insignia is placed on every bottle of Ontario wine that is chosen by a panel of carefully chosen wine professionals, indicating it has reached the high-quality standards set by the VQA.

The VQA was formally recognized in 1989 by the Ontario government and is now run by a board of directors consisting of volunteers from the wineries, grape growers, the LCBO and research institutions.

It's not surprising that the consumer quickly recognized the high quality of VQA wines to such an extent that each year there is still an insufficient volume of varietal grapes produced to meet the demand.

Not surprisingly, the larger wineries have since started producing wines for VQA standards to ensure that their wineries obtain recognition, albeit a very small quantity compared to their total production. The important fact is that the VQA movement has increased all winemaking standards in Canada, and the consumer is well served by this organization.

The next major step is to achieve recognition by the Canadian federal government for the various designated viticultural areas—Niagara Peninsula, Pelee Island and Lake Erie North Shore—to enable VQA wines to be accepted for export to EEC countries.

Hillebrand was a very active member of the founding group of the VQA. We were able to provide meaningful input, mainly in two areas. Our European heritage and support allowed us to illustrate to the other founding members the quality standards set in the winemaking countries of Europe; and, very importantly, we worked closely with our grape growers. This was to ensure that grapes would be produced to meet the exacting standards required to carry the VQA insignia. Hillebrand was committed to the VQA movement and became the largest producer of varietal wines selected by the VQA panel. Our plant manager, Peter Gamble, went on to become the executive director of the VQA and now travels around the world promoting the wines of Ontario.

The establishment of the VQA in Ontario was for all of us at Hillebrand like a dream come true. Since the introduction of self-service liquor stores by the LCBO, wine customers had become more and more familiar with the classification of the quality standards. By learning to read wine labels, they knew the meaning on French labels of "AOC" (Appelation d'Origine Côntrolée), on Italian labels "DOC" (Denominacione di Origine Controllata), and on German labels "Qualitatswein." All of these designations meant essentially the same thing: regulated quality control. Now the new VQA symbol signified that certain Ontario wines met standards of quality.

John Swan, one of the founding members of the VQA, organized lectures, given by himself and Ben Huchin, for the staff of Hillebrand's Wine Information Centre. In order to be able to inform the public, staff had to understand the criteria used in wine classifications in other countries and to compare these with VQA designations. John organized similar lectures for the staff of our 42 wine stores. Slowly the web of information was spreading to the public at large.

Our Wine Information Centre was visited by thousands of visitors and numerous organized tour groups, an increase of 72 percent over the previous year. John Swan decided to keep the center open throughout the winter months, and the tours thronged to the winery year-round. Our new facilities for wine seminars were booked weeks ahead and were used by universities, the media and wine clubs. In 1988 Hillebrand's Wine Information Centre was included in the

Ontario government tourism brochure. After lobbying the government, other wineries offering tours were included in this brochure.

Hillebrand worked in tandem with Peter Mielzynski Agencies to promote and explain the significance of VQA designation. While calling at LCBO stores, agency representatives took the opportunity to explain the meaning of VQA classification to store personnel. They found that the VQA symbol, awarded to many of Hillebrand's varietal wines, also helped to convince restaurant buyers to add those wines to their lists. It took time and a great deal of work to promote the VQA designation, but the effort paid dividends to both the Ontario wine industry and the Ontario grape growers.

A legislative change also helped the process. After three years of intensive negotiations with the government of Ontario and its liquor control board, wine tastings were finally permitted in Ontario retail wine stores. Hillebrand offered its first official tasting on October 21, 1988, at Ottawa's Rideau Centre Hillebrand wine store. Ottawa mayor James A. Durrell and Hillebrand's John Swan were in attendance to cut the ribbon to launch the new tasting. John received a special letter from Prime Minister Brian Mulroney, extending best wishes for Hillebrand's first tasting. The letter was presented and read during the tasting ceremony by the legislative assistant to Niagara Falls, MP Rob Nicholson, in whose riding Hillebrand Winery was located.

John Swan decided to offer wine tasting in only 12 stores initially. Gradually, during the next two years, the rest of the stores would acquire wine-tasting facilities. Hillebrand staff had to undergo extensive training to prepare them for hosting wine tastings. Training included seminars with Ben Huchin, Greg Berti and other experts. Hillebrand staff had to acquire a thorough knowledge of all aspects of winemaking so that they could speak with confidence about the wines being tasted and so that they could introduce and explain to customers the meaning of the Vintners Quality Alliance classification.

9

POLITICS AND THE WINE INDUSTRY

he major campaign issue of the election that Brian Mulroney had called for on November 21, 1988, was free trade. If the Conservatives won, approval of NAFTA by both houses of parliament would be assured. In the end, the Conservatives did win.

The grape growers, the wineries and the Ontario government had always been closely involved in mapping out the future directions of the wine industry. In 1988 the Wine Content Act, under the direction of the Ministry of Agriculture, was changed to prevent the use of any wines made from Labrusca grapes. At the same time, the quantity of wine that could be produced from a ton of grapes was reduced by 20 percent to 818 liters (213 gal.). This drastically affected the wineries (mainly the larger companies) that relied on maximizing the amount of juice obtained to provide a healthy bottom line without a great deal of consideration to quality. This new act came about from the lobbying efforts of Hillebrand and other quality-minded wineries.

In 1988, the GATT (General Agreement on Tariffs and Trade) ruling on unfair trade advantages due to lower markups, coupled with NAFTA, forced changes in the attitudes of the owners of the wineries.

The free trade agreement with the United States was the catalyst in removing the preferential treatment provided to the Ontario wine and grape industries. Up until then, the Ontario wineries had benefited a differential of 65 percent over other Canadian and all imported wines, that is, the markup was 65 percent lower. But the free trade agreement called for the markup on U.S. imported wines to be reduced by 50 percent by January 1, 1990, and over the next five years to be equal to that of Canadian wines.

The most profound aspect of this deal was that it spurred European wine producers to strongly lobby their governments to take action over the preferential markups applied to Canadian wines and U.S. wines sold in Canada. Member countries of the European Economic Community (EEC) banded together and complained that all provincial liquor boards broke the GATT regulations by implementing higher markups on their imported wines. The federal trade minister, John Crosby, put together a team of negotiators in the fall of 1988 who met in Brussels with their EEC counterparts. The wineries, through the Wine Council of Ontario (WCO), had hurriedly put together a paper outlining reasons for keeping the status quo. The main thrust of their argument was that various European wine-producing countries were themselves providing heavy subsidies to support the export of their wines, including those shipped to Canada.

As is often the case, when it comes to negotiations between international bodies, rational arguments fell by the wayside. The WCO paper was completely disregarded, and in the face of retaliatory action, such as the Europeans threatening to ban the import of Canadian lumber, a deal was agreed upon, which included equalizing the Liquor Board markups between the European and Canadian wines, over a period of 10 years. Up until then Canadian wines were marked up lower than imported wines. There was no parallel agreement to reduce the subsidies in European wine-producing regions.

The government of Ontario was apprehensive about the loss of profits to the LCBO, which would result from the lowering of markups. They, therefore, implemented a sliding scale whereby Ontario wine markups would gradually increase to match those of imported wines. This plan was to be implemented over seven years in the case of U.S. wines, and 10 years for all other imported wines.

Ontario wineries and grape growers were naturally very concerned as to how their wine would compete over the transition period. Both the Ontario Grape Growers' Marketing Board and the WCO lobbied the Ontario government and the federal government to make the case that the industry was in real need of support to remain in business.

The need to produce wines to compete with imported products resulted in new regulations lowering the amount of wine that could be produced from a ton of grapes. This, combined with NAFTA and GATT changes, convinced many wineries, especially larger operations, that the industry would collapse. These grape growers possessed hundreds of acres of undesirable vines that, together with the wineries' lack of experience and financial clout, made it virtually impossible for them to compete with imports on an equal basis.

Many meetings were held with the various players in the wine industry and Ontario's provincial Liberal government departments. The Ministry of Corporate and Consumer Relations, Agriculture, and Finance were involved in exploring methods to restructure the industry so that it would be competitive in the future. The farming community of growers provided the strongest political clout. They were vocal about the loss of agricultural land due to the "sellout" by the provincial and federal governments in their negotiations with the United States and the EEC. Ontario premier David Peterson set up an emergency committee of the various ministries to work out a plan to salvage the vineyards.

After many days of negotiations a deal was struck between the growers, the wine producers, the Ontario government and the federal government. Part of the agreement was in the form of a program to invest more than $150 million in the industry in the next five years. The Ontario government would recoup much of this sum from the increased markups being levied on Ontario wines due to the GATT agreement. An important aspect of the Ontario package, which amounted to $48 million, went in reimbursements to farmers for pulling out the Labrusca and other unwanted grape varieties. The number of vineyards planted in Ontario was reduced from 9,600 to 6,800 hectares (24,000 to 17,000 acres) due to the "pull-out" program. As a result, farmers received just under $7,000 per hectare and were left still owning the land. This caused some friction between farmers content with the status quo and those who had had the foresight to already remove Labrusca and replant with grape varieties in demand.

Another part of the agreement was to supply the growers with what became the Grape Price Support Program. Under the new Wine Content Act, Labrusca grapes were prevented from being used in table wine. However, the wineries were legally bound to purchase these grapes each year until the year 2000. This came to 22,950 metric tons (25,500 tons) of grapes from Ontario farmers, consisting of hybrid and vinifera grapes.

The Grape Price Support Program paid farmers a subsidy on the difference between the value of a ton of a grape variety grown locally, compared to that grown in California. The Ontario Grape Growers' Marketing Board negotiated the price of every grape variety each year with Ontario wineries. If a variety was priced higher than a variety grown in California, the farmer received the difference under this program. The program ensured that the wineries were able to purchase the enforced 22,950 metric tons (25,500 tons) a year at the prices paid by California wineries; and the wineries were able to purchase at a competitive price. This program gave the growers 12 years to become competitive with foreign growers.

As part of the assistance program, the wineries received funds to improve their production facilities and to market their wines. A winery had to provide a credible proposal, explaining in detail how the funds would assist them in becoming more competitive. Normally, the winery was required to invest matching dollars to qualify for the program. It also had to provide guarantees to the government, including performance-related clauses.

Nineteen eighty-eight was a crucial year for the Ontario wine industry. Due to the determination of the growers, wineries and government, the challenges were mostly met. In one year, the industry had dealt with the introduction of the new VQA body, Wine Content Act changes and the international rulings of NAFTA and GATT.

At Hillebrand Estates Winery, we were pleased with the changes made by the Wine Content Act, as this was the direction to which we were already committed. We were not in the slightest affected by the ban on Labrusca grapes, as we had only used high-quality hybrid and vinifera grapes. Our grape growers were already producing to meet our requirements, so they were not affected by the changes in an adverse way. In fact, they gained from the new Grape Price Support Program.

We were pleased that the industry had been forced to take notice of the effect of markup changes. It meant that the industry would become more competitive in terms of quality, price and image. We were under some pressure at Hillebrand due to the markup changes, as they had lowered our contributors' margins, but we were not affected as much as many other wineries, since the markups did not apply to wine sold through our own stores.

The 1988 vintage time was almost upon us, and our winemaking team, Greg Berti, Ben Huchin and Robert Mielzynski, was anxious to inaugurate the newly built press house. Our grape growers were producing better qualities of grapes. The canopy management, including shoot positioning and leaf removal around the developing bunches, was one example of the viticultural techniques that the most forward-thinking grape growers employed in their vineyards. The resulting varietals were second to none.

The time had come to take advantage of key vineyard sites, maturing vines and our advanced winemaking skills. In keeping with European tradition we saw that the soil was as important as the grape. The French and Italians name their wines after their châteaux, castellos and vineyards. The specific location and region of the châteaux, castellos or vineyards tells the story of the wine in the bottle and gives it its pedigree. It is true that Europe had generations of tradition to build on; nevertheless, we felt that Hillebrand was ready to produce a wine series and a brand name that reflected the maturity of the winery. The answer lay with the Trius concept. Trius was to embody a fusion of art and technology in three distinct steps—the "trio of steps" in wine's evolution—the cultivating and harvesting of the grapes, the winemaking and finally the marketing.

Our viticulturist, Greg Berti, was working closely with the leading growers in three key regions of the Niagara grape-growing area: the Queenston region, the Lakefront region and the Beamsville Bench region.

The Queenston region, where the lime-based soil was heaviest, had the warmest climate and produced grapes that were high in sugar. The resulting wines were full-bodied and fruity. At that time, Huebel Vineyard was the leading grower in the area. Their Chardonnay was the envy of the region.

The Lakefront region, with its sandy soil and exposure to the breezes of Lake Ontario, yielded grapes that were higher in acidity but also high in sugar content. The resulting wines were more delicate due to the acids, and they showed elegant flavors after fermentation. The Buis vineyard was the leader in this region.

The Beamsville Bench region, along the Niagara Escarpment to the west of St. Catharines, proved to be a wonderful region with lime-based soils. The vineyards in this area benefited from the cooling breezes of Lake Ontario. The resulting wines were complex, full-bodied and rich in good acids. We used Lenko and Schoemaker Vineyards, as well as several other growers in this area.

The personality of each "terroir" was starting to express itself. Greg Berti set the standards required for the quality needed for the Trius wines. The growers had to follow specific methods of planting, pruning, thinning, leaf management, spraying and picking. This was achieved through Greg's determination to produce quality Chardonnay, Cabernet Sauvignon, Merlot, Cabernet Franc and Riesling. The end result—superior varietals derived from selected vineyard sites, the first step in the birth of the Trius concept.

Ben and Robert closely watched the work that was being done by Greg and the growers. By choosing, together with the growers, the very best location within each grower's farm, they could plan for the harvest. Their combined experience told them that the improved viticulture would ensure the success of Trius.

The grapes were under control, but Ben and Robert felt that the program required certain enhancements. They had chosen the best of the best, which included mature vines and ripe grapes. In the French vineyards only the best grapes of specific varietals can support oak barrels. Generally speaking, the better the vineyard site the more oak is possible, although these conclusions require experimental verification. With this in mind, Ben and Robert went to France to find the right match for their wines. For the Chardonnay they chose oak from the forests of Allier and Troncais. With the use of dripping tanks and light pressing, the juices were fermented in these new oak barrels and left on the lees. This "stirring on the lees" method, where yeast is deposited in the barrel, creates a fuller, rounder style of wine. Every vintage makes the winemaker! Especially with Trius, experience and creativity were crucial. Each of the three vineyard sites produced close to 500 cases of Chardonnay in 1989, an indication of the dedication to an extremely limited quantity of truly superior wine.

A high-quality red wine is more difficult to produce in the Niagara region. Whereas white wines are made largely from juice alone, the essence of a quality Bordeaux-style red is derived from a combination of the skins and juice. The fermentation time is longer and fermentation on the skins obligatory. This extra variable plays more into the hands of nature. More elements in the recipe required the judicious control of winemaking. This tradition of blending grapes in Bordeaux goes back to the seventeenth century and represents part of the mystique that is Bordeaux. Ben and Robert were convinced that the quality white grapes could be grown successfully, but the red varietals only in exceptional vintages. The Trius red could be released only if the quality was excellent.

A rigorous grape selection process was established for the reds. As with Chardonnay, key vineyard sites were chosen and the best grapes selected. Ben and Robert were convinced that, under the right conditions, they could produce a top-class Trius red. They had the advantage of the new press house, and with the new technology they could obtain good results. The winemakers were able to extract the finest juices from the grapes with the use of a Vinimatic Tank where, through controlled temperature and pressure, the grapes yielded their precious color and flavor to maximum effect. To maximize control, the winemakers fermented each varietal in a separate vat and then selected the batches to be blended after rigorous tastings and numerous rejections.

Concerned with quality, Ben and Robert again traveled to the coopers in France to purchase the most suitable barrels. Trius Red was developed on the traditional methods as practiced in Bordeaux (the Bordelais method), creating a blended wine based on Cabernet Sauvignon, Merlot and Cabernet Franc. Trius Red was limited to a mere 800 cases in its first vintage of 1989—evidence of the rigorous selection process involved.

Riesling from Niagara, when drunk fairly young, is one of the most enjoyable wines. Trius Riesling was chosen as the third wine in the series because of the high quality of Riesling grapes from all three regions of Niagara. The key factor when choosing these grapes is high acidity, which is needed to maintain a fresh component. This,

From left to right: Emil Underberg; Jim Bradley, M.P.P. St. Catherines; the author, Peter Mielzynski-Zychlinski; John Swan; and Jack Ackroyd, chairman of the Liquor Control Board of Ontario, at the opening ceremonies of Hillebrand's new facilities in 1987.

Hillebrand's winemaking team with Europress and Vinimatic. Left to right: Peter Gamble, Heinz Turk, Andreas Gestaltner and John Swan.

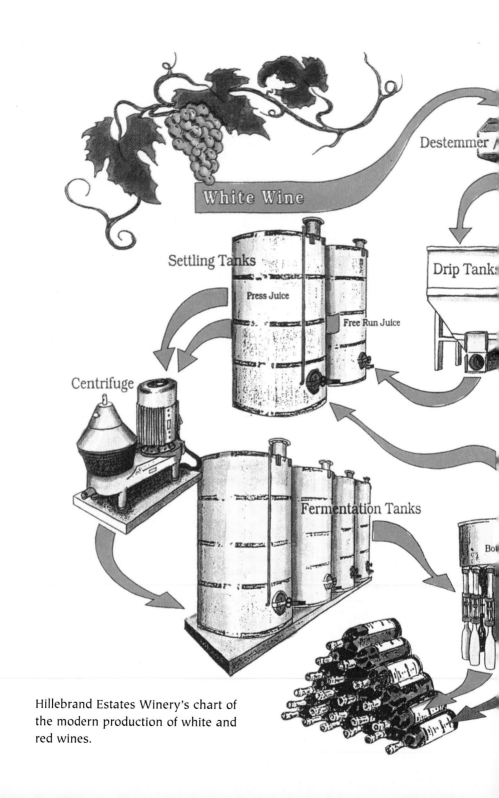

Hillebrand Estates Winery's chart of the modern production of white and red wines.

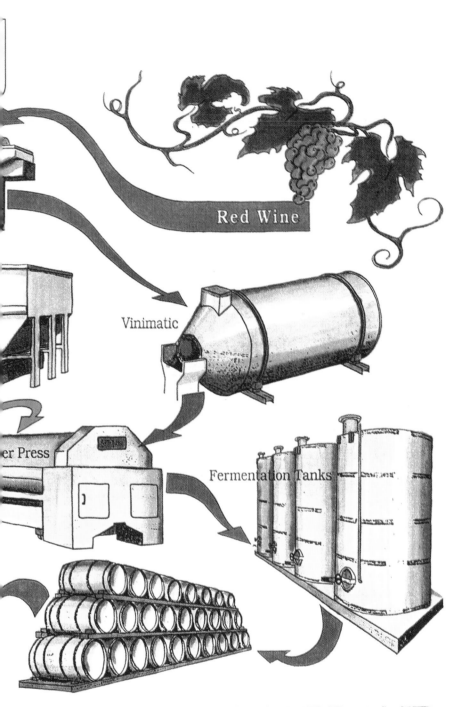

Red Wine

Vinimatic

er Press

Fermentation Tanks

HILLEBRAND
ESTATES WINERY

The staff of Hillebrand Estates Winery photographed in front of the winery's main building in 1986.

Hillebrand's commitment to quality is widely recognized through its many international awards and tributes.

At the International Wine and Spirit Competition in Surrey, England, Helmuth van Schellenbeck (left), Director of Underberg Co., Switzerland, receives, on behalf of Hillebrand, the award for our Riesling Classic. Mr. Drouhin, of Maison Joseph Drouhin, is shown presenting the award.

together with the correct sugar levels, would give the wine balance and finesse. Ben and Robert used small 10,000-liter (2,600-gal.) chilling tanks to ensure the fermentation remained at a constant temperature. The resulting product, Trius Riesling, showed a delicate hint of fruit, with a full dry flavor. The initial concern was that the wine was a little too dry or austere. Ultimately, both Ben and Robert decided that this would prove an advantage, giving the true, elegant Riesling character an opportunity to express itself. Trius Riesling proved to be a distinguished addition to the Trius family.

The Trius wine program was ready, but the packaging and marketing that would reflect the wine quality was yet to be finalized. This was the final but crucial step—the introduction of Trius to the market. The series was a total departure from anything that had thus far been developed. Trius had to symbolize the fruits of our labor at Hillebrand and also stand as a beacon for the Niagara wine-growing region. Robert, who had one foot in the vineyards and another in design and marketing, rose to the occasion. In his mind the Trius concept required a clear departure from the past. He envisioned a separate bottle shape for each of the three Trius wines. The bottles he selected were made of dark olive-colored glass, with extra-long necks. They were visually unforgettable.

Our production manager, Scott Moore, was not entirely happy with these developments, as he had to find a way to bottle the wines in odd-sized bottles. However beautiful these bottles were, they were also a nightmare for the bottling line. Scott, resourceful as ever, found a way.

To finish the bottle, special corks were required, longer than usual and adapted to the width of the bottlenecks. Ben and Robert did not use plastic capsules but devised a system of pouring special colored wax to seal the bottles. The wax looked very attractive and, for the ecologically minded consumer, this was much better than capsules. The plan was to change the color of the wax for every vintage.

The next phase was the labels and the key visual design. Each wine would have a specially designed etched label, like an engraving. The brand name, Trius, appeared in its own style of calligraphy. The labels presented three images of the three stages of winemaking: a woman picking the grapes, which represented viticulture; a winemaker pressing the grapes, which represented the winemaking stage; and a girl serving the finished, marketed product. The design used only three colors—the basic white for the label itself, and black and mustard-orange for the inscriptions and the images. These beautiful, artisan labels embraced the tall, slender stylish bottles.

The creation of Trius was a very expensive project. Every step required extreme care in the use of the finest products. From the very beginning, Trius wines sold very well. Their superior quality was immediately recognized by Ontario's wine critics. Greg, Ben and Robert put their full efforts into the making of this wine, and its success was their greatest reward! The numerous accolades Trius received were a testament to their achievement.

Over the preceding years, Ontario-produced Eiswein had become the flagship of Canadian wines. In 1983, Hillebrand was the first winery in Ontario to produce Eiswein. Our Eiswein was packaged in the traditional German 375-mL (13-oz.) hoch, a slim style of bottle, and the label was designed to reflect the original German style. In 1988, with the introduction of the Vintners Quality Alliance, when the Trius series was being developed, the management at Hillebrand thought that it was the right time to introduce a new package for its Eiswein.

While Robert was in Italy looking for suitable bottles for the Trius series, he also found the unique bottle for our Eiswein. The change from the hoch bottle to this tall, elegant bottle gave a new face to this already distinguished and well-known wine. Robert understood the importance of the complete mix for marketing success: superb-quality wine in an inviting package with a striking label design. He brought these ideas together to assure that the new Hillebrand Eiswein package would be ready for the 1990 vintage.

As mentioned previously, the extremely dry weather conditions of spring 1988 caused great stress to the vineyards. But then the rains came in late July. The summer was also warmer than usual, with 10 percent more sunshine than the norm. A cool, dry fall provided ideal ripening conditions for the grapes. As a result of these exceptional, new conditions the vintage of 1988 was considered to be the finest on record.

The Niagara Peninsula boasts a climate and growing soil that is comparable to the finest wine-producing areas in the world. Vineyard consultant Greg Berti was able to select a balance of grapes from both escarpment vineyards, where a constant air flow prevents frost damage, combined with grapes from the lakeshore vineyards, where a moderating effect allows for substantial acidity. This combination gave the winemakers the fruits to produce one of the finest Niagara Chardonnays that year.

Harvesting of the 1988 Chardonnay grapes started on September 21 and continued for 10 days. There was abundant sunshine throughout September, with slightly below-normal temperatures and precipitation during harvest. Greg felt that the high-quality fruit was the best of the decade.

In producing Hillebrand's 1988 Chardonnay, which was accredited with VQA status, careful handling of the grapes was crucial. Free-run juice was separated into different tanks. Cold fermentation lasted several weeks in order to achieve the finest fruit characteristics possible. The initial fermentation was followed by malolactic fermentation (a process that involves converting the malic acid to a mellower lactic acid). Throughout the year, approximately 15 of the chosen wines were barrel aged to create an elegant balance in the 1988 Chardonnay. In addition to making great strides with Chardonnay, Hillebrand had great successes with many other varietals.

Nineteen eighty-eight was an extremely successful year in the continued positive growth of the winery. The company experienced a sales increase of almost 40 percent over 1987: LCBO stores had sold 71,530 cases, Hillebrand retail stores 98,200, and 7,380 cases were exported, making a total of 177,110 cases. It was interesting to note the increasing importance of the Hillebrand retail stores for the winery. From the total of 21,000 cases of varietal wines sold during 1988, only 4,500 cases were sold through the LCBO stores. Unfortunately, we had to short-ship Chardonnay, as, in spite of the incredible progress attained by the grape growers, the supply of grapes was not adequate to meet the ever-increasing demand for that wine.

In 1988, Hillebrand became the top award-winning winery in Canada. These awards were achieved not only in Canadian competitions but also in international events. Here are a few of the highlights:

International Eastern Wine Competition (U.S.)

Eiswein, 1986 ~ *Silver Medal*
Late Harvest Vidal, 1987 ~ *Silver Medal*
Canadian Champagne ~ *Bronze Medal*
Kir Royale ~ *Bronze Medal*
Pinot Noir, 1987 ~ *Bronze Medal*
Maréchal Foch, 1987 ~ *Quality Wine Award*

Intervin International Competition (U.S.)

Eiswein, 1986 ~ *Gold Medal*
Canadian Champagne ~ *Silver Medal*
Collectors' Choice Chardonnay, 1986 ~ *Silver Medal*
Kir Royale ~ *Bronze Medal*

We were particularly pleased that our Eiswein (1986) was awarded a gold medal at the Intervin International Competition and a silver medal at the International Eastern Wine Competition in the United States.

To ensure the continuance of the highest-quality Eiswein, a new electrically powered press was purchased. This enabled the winemakers to maintain consistent pressure. Until then the Eiswein press had been manually operated. One of Hillebrand's mottos was: "No matter how successful a brand, there is always room for improvement."

The new press house was working to capacity, promising more successes for the future. Our winemakers, Ben Huchin and Robert Mielzynski, had chosen a special selection of wines for oak barrel fermentation and ageing. The results of the 1988 vintage would be appraised in 1989, 1990 and 1991. Meanwhile, the winery and the grape growers were looking forward with great optimism toward further achievements in 1989.

10

THE VINTAGE CLUB IS BORN

With the advent of free trade we anticipated that the LCBO would import much larger quantities of California varietal wines. NAFTA called for the former markup on U.S. imported wines to be reduced by 50 percent by January 1, 1990. Then, over the following five years, the markup would become equal to that of Canada's domestic wines. In anticipation of these developments, Hillebrand Estates Winery had been building a direct relationship with its customers through its own stores.

By 1990 Hillebrand would have 51 retail stores in operation. Well-organized and staffed by educated personnel, they provided wine tastings and valued information to our customers. Projections showed that by 1990 our grape growers would, for the first time, have sufficient produce to meet our demands, and consequently, Hillebrand Harvest Chardonnay, the fastest-selling Chardonnay in Ontario, would not be out of stock.

The real competition with California wines was expected to play out in the LCBO stores and the restaurant trade. Peter Mielzynski Agencies continued to do excellent work promoting Hillebrand wines both in the LCBO and in restaurants. Hillebrand and the agency worked closely together to prepare new promotions for Hillebrand wines. At the same time Robert was working with a well-known Canadian art director, Rene Schoepflin, to develop new labels for Hillebrand's Harvest Wines line. John wanted distinct designs and colors on the new labels of different varietals so that they would stand out from the competition at LCBO stores. The 1988 vintage of Chardonnays and Rieslings was released in 1989 with the newly designed labels, light brown for the Chardonnays and green for the Rieslings.

We were in the ideal situation to communicate directly to our customers, through our ever-expanding network of retail stores, but we needed to be able to do more for them to secure their loyalty to Hillebrand. Consequently, we developed the Hillebrand Estates Winery Vintage Club in 1989, to convey wine education and details of special wines to club members. Christine Colby was appointed to spearhead this exciting program. Christine had developed a good understanding of our concepts since she had worked very successfully in our Wine Information Centre.

A club member would receive:

- our newsletter, *Inside Wine*, quarterly, which provided knowledge on the latest developments in viticulture and winemaking;

- offers of prereleases of new vintages at special rates, back vintages and limited quantity (single-vineyard) wines;

- invitations to Hillebrand's winemaker events throughout Ontario;

- exclusive visits to the winery, including a seminar on the pairing of food and wines;

- connoisseur wine accessories;

- a member's kit, including a file for recording personal wine-tasting notes.

The Vintage Club became very popular and attracted more than 4,000 members in the first two years.

Meanwhile in Vienna, our sister company, the Schlumberger Winery, had bought P.M. Mounier & Company. Founded in the nineteenth century, in France, P.M. Mounier was a well-established winery producing high-quality sparkling wine in the traditional *méthode champenoise.* Schlumberger Sparkling House itself had almost 200 years of expertise in producing champagne, so this was a dynamic pairing. Emil Underberg knew that the Niagara grape-growing area was producing excellent varietal wines, most notably based on Chardonnay and Pinot Noir grape varieties, which both make very fine sparkling wines. With this in mind, he decided to build a Mounier cellar at Hillebrand. The winery, which was then in the process of building a barrel cellar next to the new production and office building, consolidated the two costs, and a Mounier and ageing cellar were built at the same time.

The roots of *méthode champenoise* are traceable to a technique developed in France three hundred years ago. By fermenting "in the bottle," the French had discovered that a finer series of bubbles and more discreet flavors resulted. This process was very expensive and capital-intensive. It required a series of steps—riddling (moving the deposits of yeast in the bottle), disgorging (removing yeast from the bottle), and adding a liqueur d'expédition (sugar dissolved in wine to help sweeten the final product). This classical method is the most labor-intensive and costly but can produce sublime results.

There are two other less expensive methods of making sparkling wines. Hillebrand was already producing the Canadian Champagne and Riesling Cuvée, using *méthode Charmat,* also known as *méthode cuvée close.* The Charmat process works by adding yeast to the wine in a large pressure tank. The second fermentation transforms the still wine into a sparkling wine. Using *méthode Charmat* is less labor-intensive than the traditional bottle fermentation of *méthode champenoise* wines. The process can, however, produce excellent sparkling wine. Hillebrand's Canadian Champagne, created using this method, won many awards in international competitions.

The other most popular and least costly method, not used by Hillebrand but by some large wineries in Canada, involves the pumping of carbon dioxide into the still wine, which is then bottled under pressure.

At that time in Ontario there were only three wineries using the *méthode champenoise* in their production of sparkling wines: Podamer, Inniskillin and Château des Charmes. The addition of the Mounier cellar gave Hillebrand a distinct advantage. The newly built underground Mounier cellar was especially designed to age more than 400,000 bottles. A confidence booster, this $2 million investment by Underberg provided new direction for the winery.

Schlumberger's master blender and manager, Heinz Turk, supervised the development of Mounier in Canada. My son Robert became Mounier's coordinator. He had apprenticed at Schlumberger Winery under Heinz's supervision, and John Swan could depend on his abilities.

An extract from our newsletter, *Inside Wine*, tells the history of the Mounier method of making champagne:

The legend goes that the forefather of all cellarers was a Benedictine monk living in the 17th century. He was able to select the best wines for a blend when tasting the freshly picked grapes. Mounier has made sure that particular tradition of quality has endured. Purity is the result of meticulous care at the earliest stage of winemaking—the growing of grapes in the vineyards. The same meticulous care holds true for the selection and pressing of the grapes for vinification. Through fermentation they turn into high quality Chardonnay and Pinot Noir wines worthy of becoming part of the Mounier blend.

Since Hillebrand's varietal wines had won top honors in European competitions, and Canadian wine lovers were especially taken with our Chardonnay, we were sure that the Canadian market was ready for the *méthode champenoise* sparkling Chardonnay and Pinot Noir varieties.

Greg Berti, who by now knew the Niagara Peninsula intimately, worked with grape growers to identify the best areas from which to select the grapes for the new sparkling wines. The Lakeshore region proved ideal as it produced grapes of higher acidity and lower brix, while maintaining the ripe flavors necessary for the production of *méthode champenoise* sparkling wine. The greatest care had to be taken in picking the grapes by hand and transporting them to the winery in baskets so as not to bruise them.

An exact harvest schedule was of the utmost importance to help ensure the microbiological cleanliness of the harvested grapes. A prolonged harvest date can cause contamination of the grapes, such as bacterial and fungal infestations, resulting in a buildup of histamine. The grape growers understood these nuances and Hillebrand's pursuit of quality. They also shared our commitment to a successful launch of the first cuvée (a blend of wines to produce a particular style of finished wine) for the *méthode champenoise* Canadian Mounier production.

As soon as the handpicked Chardonnay grapes arrived at our press house, the de-stemmer separated the stems from the grapes. The grapes were then directed to the drip tanks. The natural weight of the grapes upon themselves provided a 60 percent recovery of the highest quality free-run juice. Once the juice was fed through the drip tank, it was then clarified through the new centrifuge. From here, the juice was pumped through the pipes into the fermenting vats. Pinot Noir grapes went through the same procedure, and the juice was pumped into separate fermenting vats. Ben and Robert carefully monitored the entire harvest and cellaring.

The next stage of the *méthode champenoise* process was the controlled fermentation. To carry out the ideal fermentation of the must, selected natural yeast strains were added, to limit the buildup of histamines. The temperature was kept at 18°C (64°F), resulting in high-quality wines with the lowest histamine levels. During every production stage, the histamine levels were constantly analyzed by Ben in our Hillebrand Quality Control Laboratory, a facility that was designed to enable tests on the wine at every level of production. Once the first fermentation was finished, the wine was clarified by cold stabilization, that is, it was cooled down to control stability during filtration, and then filtered, to be ready for the next stage.

Hillebrand's experienced group of tasters assembled to decide the process of making the cuvée for the second fermentation of Mounier, which would take place inside the bottles. They all realized that they had to rely on taste, sight and smell to determine the right proportion of each of the still wines produced for the cuvée, which would reflect the flavor profile and specific character of Mounier Brut from Vienna. They agreed to produce 33,360 liters (8,736 gal.) of cuvée, using 23 percent Pinot Noir, 65 percent Chardonnay and 12 percent of 1987 vintage Riesling. The number of liters would correspond to 44,480 bottles.

The characteristically shaped Mounier bottles were imported from Vienna. These green bottles, made from a special thick glass in order to withstand pressure equivalent to 6 kilogram-force per square centimeter (80 pounds per square inch), added considerably to production expenses. Hillebrand's plant manager, Scott Moore, assembled a special bottling line for the Mounier production.

The natural yeast strains, developed by the Underberg Laboratories in Switzerland and yielding near-zero histamine, were added, with the *liqueur de tirage* (sugar dissolved in wine to help with second fermentation), to the cuvée in the bottles, which were then tightly sealed with crown caps (stoppers). The bottles were placed on their sides with the bottlenecks toward the wall. Row upon row, stacked 2 meters high, they formed a massive structure. We waited at least three months for the first sign of a bubble. The ageing time, in a temperature-controlled cellar (usually 12°C [54°F]) takes from 12 to 18 months.

This was the first time the Mounier *méthode champenoise* was being used in Canada. Consequently, it was difficult, even for Heinz Turk, to predict how long it would take for the cuvée in the bottles to mature. Only by a schedule of wine tastings could decisions be made as to when the *méthode champenoise* Mounier would be ready to go through the final stages. Once the ageing time was completed, the bottles, one by one, would be taken by the neck and shaken vigorously, in order to loosen up the yeast particles, which sometimes get stuck to the glass. Following this procedure, called *poignettage* (shaking), the bottles were moved to the riddling racks.

Riddling racks are used to move the deposits of yeast from the bottle into the bidule in the neck of the bottle. The bottles were loaded almost horizontally onto the racks, then turned an eighth of a turn, and gradually inclined to an almost vertical position. The yellow strip on the bottom of every Mounier bottle was an important reference when riddling the bottles. It took 24 turns to move the yeast deposit up into the neck.

The next stage, called disgorging, is the process of removing the yeast from the bottles. Before removing the crown cap, the neck of the bottle had to be frozen. The pressure within the bottle would push the ice, containing the deposits in the bidule, out of the bottle. In order to freeze the bottlenecks, Hillebrand used a special apparatus from Austria that had 41 holes and could process approximately 300 bottles per hour.

Dosage, which is the process of adding the *liqueur d'expédition*, has to be done immediately after disgorging. The amount of *liqueur d'expédition* to be added depends on whether the wine is to be a brut (the driest) or a demi-sec (semi-dry). As a rule, the best cuvée requires the least dosage. The brut was reserved for the top cuvée. Immediately after dosage, the bottles went to the corking area. Here they were corked with laminated corks and wire hoods, bearing the Mounier coat of arms, and closed firmly.

After two years of ageing, the dust and wine spoilage settled on the bottles and they had to be washed, before they were stacked up again for two more months of ageing. Only then were the bottles labeled and prepared for distribution.

While the winemaking was taking place, Robert Mielzynski, with the cooperation of Schlumberger's managing director Dr. Rudi Kobatsch's team in Austria, had developed very attractive front, back and neck labels with a gold capsule. The Mounier six-bottle case was designed specifically for display purposes. At Hillebrand's 51 stores, cases would be stacked five high, with the top cases open for better presentation. In addition, the cases themselves were designed with the Mounier logo, the *méthode champenoise* inscription and the address of the Hillebrand Estates Winery.

The production of our varietal and sparkling wines was very time-consuming. Since Robert was vice president, John Swan wanted him to be exposed to different aspects of the business while still being involved in winemaking; in particular, he wanted Robert to learn more about marketing and sales. As a result, Ben needed another winemaker to work with. He knew of a young French winemaker who might fit Hillebrand's requirements.

Jean-Laurent ("J. L.") Groux was born and raised in the famous French wine-producing region of the Loire Valley. As a young man he studied the art and technology of fine wine production in the town of Beaune, in the world-renowned wine region of Burgundy. Following three years of practical and technical training in viticulture and winemaking, Groux moved, in 1980, to the Oenology Institute of Bordeaux at the University of Bordeaux. In 1982 he was awarded the National Diploma of Oenology. Following graduation, Groux held several jobs in France. Then, with a view to gaining international experience, he toured vineyards and wineries throughout Europe and New Zealand, Argentina, Chile and the United States. In 1989 he started at Hillebrand.

Hillebrand had aroused the interest of many distinguished visitors to Canada. We were pleased to extend our hospitality by arranging special tours, wine tastings followed by lunches, and menus set according to the selection of wines chosen for the occasion. Often we took our guests to meet our grape growers and subsequently strolled through their vineyards.

One of the most enjoyable visits was that of Jean Schÿler and his daughter Sophie. Jean Schÿler was the owner of the established Maison Schröder et Schÿler, house of fine wines in Bordeaux. Peter Mielzynski Agencies were the agents for Schröder et Schÿler in Canada. Before the Second World War my family in Poland used to buy wines from Jean Schÿler's father and before that from his grandfather! While at the winery, Jean Schÿler and his daughter, accompanied by Robert, tasted several barrel samples of wines. They were particularly impressed by our Chardonnays and newly released 1987 sparkling Riesling. Jean said: "I wish you 250 years of success, which, judging from what I have tasted, seems assured." An apt sentiment since Maison Schröder et Schÿler had just celebrated their 250th anniversary.

During this period the federal government's Department of External Affairs arranged a cross-Canada tour for Thomas Luber, editor of one of Germany's leading business publications, *Industriemagazin*. He was researching West German investments in Canada and, among other areas, he visited the Niagara region. Like many Europeans, he was a connoisseur of fine wines. Since he'd heard so much about Hillebrand from the Canadian ambassador to West Germany, Thomas Delworth, who had earlier visited the winery, he specifically requested to pay a visit to the winery. Robert provided him with a firsthand look at the technology employed at

Hillebrand and a sampling of a range of varietal and sparkling wines, as well as Eiswein. Thomas Luber was delighted with Hillebrand's offerings, saying they rivaled those of France and Germany.

We were always happy to welcome visitors connected with the wine and spirit industry. Thomas Klumb, an executive of Racke International, from Mainz, West Germany, was another international colleague who toured Hillebrand. Racke was one of the largest companies in Germany, known for its wines and spirits. Thomas Klumb had often tasted Hillebrand wines during European wine competitions, and was curious to find out more about the winery and the Niagara region. Another visitor welcomed to Hillebrand was Augusto Rivelli, export director for Martini & Rossi, of Torino, Italy.

A large international group visited Hillebrand Estates Winery in late April 1989. More than 180 apprentice chefs, bakers and their instructors from Australia, Italy, Jamaica, Norway, the United States, Cuba, Britain, West Germany, Singapore, Israel and Austria, as well as from several Canadian provinces, were participating in a week-long competition in Toronto, called Taste of Canada, 1989. Our guides took them, in groups of eight, through the Hillebrand tour and tastings.

Visitors often confirmed that Hillebrand Estates Winery was becoming well known internationally and, more importantly, connoisseurs worldwide were taking Ontario wines very seriously indeed.

In 1989, Ontario's minister of culture and communications, the Honorable Lily Munro, officially launched Hillebrand's limited edition Collectors' Choice Cabernet Merlot and Chardonnay at Toronto's Arts and Letters Club. The two Group of Seven paintings from the McMichael Collection featured on the labels that year were A. Y. Jackson's *Sunlit Tapestry* and *October Lake Superior*. During the years prior to the release of these wines, Greg Berti had been able to determine the best growing areas for Cabernet Sauvignon, Merlot and the most noble of white varietals, Chardonnay.

The Arts and Letters Club was an ideal place for the launch since one of the Group of Seven, J. E. H. MacDonald, had once been its president. In addition, several artists from the Group of Seven had visited the club, and their paintings were exhibited there. Over 100 guests attended the ceremony, including the Honorable Shirley Martin, minister of transportation at the time, and member of parliament for Lincoln and St. Catharines–Brock, Mike Dietsch. Minister Munro pointed out that "The McMichael Gallery and Hillebrand Estates Winery have created a unique blend of Ontario's winemaking and visual arts." She went on to say: "Your partnership is an admirable example of the excellent results that can be achieved when cultural and private industries work together. Hillebrand's elegant, world-class wines coupled with the beautiful McMichael Gallery paintings of A. Y. Jackson make for an excellent representation of fine Ontario products."

John Swan presented Lily Munro with a selection of the newly released Collectors' Choice wines and thanked the Ontario government for its great efforts in helping to develop the wine regions of Ontario to produce competitive world-class wines.

The provincial government also participated in a more local celebration. John Watson, of Watson Vineyards, a Niagara-on-the-Lake grape grower who supplied his grapes exclusively to Hillebrand Estates Winery, was crowned Grape King at the 38th Niagara Grape and Wine Festival on September 22, 1989.

Ontario's minister of the environment, the Honorable Jim Bradley, announced that John Watson's vineyards were judged the best in Niagara by research specialists from the Horticultural Research Station of Ontario in Vineland. As the Grape King, the 50-year-old John Watson was to serve as an ambassador for Ontario's grape and wine industry for the next year. He was ideally suited for the task. For many years he had grown high-quality vinifera and French hybrid varieties on his

11 hectares (28 acres) of vineyards. The vinifera varieties included Chardonnay, Riesling, Gewürztraminer, Cabernet Sauvignon and Pinot Noir. The hybrids included Seyval Blanc, Vidal and Villard Noir.

To the news that an exclusive Hillebrand grower had been crowned Grape King, Hillebrand's president, John Swan, said that he was delighted: "In accepting John Watson's grapes for our quality wines, we knew he was one of Niagara's finest growers. Now the whole industry will be aware of it. Mr. Watson knows that quality wines start in the vineyards, and we all wish him well throughout his reign as Niagara Grape King."

As a result of contributions by quality-minded producers like John Watson, Hillebrand Estates Winery continued to win awards in international competitions:

The 1989 International Eastern Wine Competition in New York received 1,702 entries representing 396 wineries from 18 different countries. Hillebrand won nine medals:

Vidal, 1988 ～ *Gold Medal*
Riesling, 1988 ～ *Silver Medal*
Seyval Blanc, 1988 ～ *Silver Medal*
Eiswein, 1987 ～ *Bronze Medal*
Canadian Champagne ～ *Bronze Medal*
Chardonnay, 1988 ～ *Bronze Medal*
Late Harvest Vidal, 1988 ～ *Bronze Medal*
Maréchal Foch, 1987 ～ *Bronze Medal*
Cream Sherry ～ *Bronze Medal*

Intervin International Competition (Canada–U.S.)

Eiswein, 1987 ⁓ *Gold Medal*
(tied for top Canadian wine and won Double Bronze for being
third-highest scoring wine in the overall competition)
Late Harvest Vidal, 1987 ⁓ *Silver Medal*
Collectors' Choice Chardonnay, 1987 ⁓ *Silver Medal*
Riesling Cuvée Sparkling, 1987 ⁓ *Bronze Medal*
Limited Edition Barrel-Fermented Chardonnay, 1988 ⁓ *Bronze Medal*
Riesling Classic, 1988 ⁓ *Bronze Medal*

International Wine and Spirit Competition (U.K.)

Eiswein, 1987 ⁓ *Silver Medal*
Late Harvest Vidal, 1987 ⁓ *Bronze Medal*
Vidal, 1987 ⁓ *Bronze Medal*
Cabernet Merlot, 1987 ⁓ *Bronze Medal*
Canadian Champagne ⁓ *Bronze Medal*

In 1989 Hillebrand was the top producer of varietal wines in Canada, winning more awards than any other winery in the country.

11

THE END OF AN ERA

*A*t the beginning of each year we held a meeting to discuss our sales, marketing, advertising and production programs. The first week of January 1990 was typical of other years as we assembled in John Swan's office to review our short- and long-term programs.

We noted that during the previous 10 years the Niagara grape-growing region had witnessed many changes. Many growers had pulled the North American grape varieties to replace them with classical varieties. The 10-year contracts from Hillebrand had helped in this regard. Nevertheless, Hillebrand faced some increased competition from the new wineries that were springing up in the Niagara region. At first, these wineries had produced a limited selection of wines, but now each one was trying to develop its unique style of good-quality wines. In addition, these new estate wineries had opened up their own winery stores, and organized wine tastings and winery tours. The increased competition was a double-edged sword; it helped Hillebrand to be located in a region that was becoming internationally recognized for its quality wineries, but on the other hand we had to find a way of distinguishing ourselves from other wineries. At our January 1990 meeting, we discussed how to go about doing this.

At that time, Hillebrand tours attracted more visitors than any other winery in the Niagara region. We had excellent educational facilities, and every year we were able to provide something new. In 1990 we planned to open the newly finished temperature- and humidity-controlled barrel ageing cellar to our tours. Visitors would view 250 barrels of different ageing wines. Two displays were arranged, the Barrel Making and the Cork Production, with appropriate pictures and samples of the different types of oak used for barrel production and the bark used for cork production. Every visitor also received a booklet that included articles written by our winemakers and viticulturist.

Following a visit to our barrel ageing cellar, the tour moved to the dark, cool Mounier cellar. There, our guests learned about the elaborate process of making Mounier using *méthode champenoise* (see page 20).

The plan was to build a special viewing room on the second floor for the tours to see, from above, the bottling lines in operation, since most people seemed to be fascinated by the process. Hillebrand had installed a third state-of-the-art line at a cost of $500,000. The new line was capable of running 120 bottles a minute; our old bottling line could fill only 40 bottles a minute.

Another event helped maximize the positive influence of our winery tours in 1990. The Regional Niagara's Retail Business Holidays Act Special Committee had given approval to Sunday openings for on-site winery stores in Niagara. The legislation provided for opening every Sunday except Easter Sunday, or when Christmas Day, Boxing Day or New Year's Day fell on a Sunday.

The move was seen as a big plus for Niagara's agriculture and tourism industries. In the past, tourists had frequently stopped by the wineries on Sundays for tours and tastings, only to find the wineries closed. The Sunday-openings legislation could not have happened at a better time for Hillebrand Estates Winery, given our plan to expand our tours.

Early in 1990 we noticed an increased interest, from both the Ontario and federal governments, in the wine industry. Finally there were signs that they believed that Canadian wines could compete success-fully with imported wines. The establishment of the Vintners Quality Alliance had certainly helped in this regard. On January 25, three government of Ontario deputy ministers and the president and chief executive officer of the Ontario Development Corporation visited selected wineries in an effort to learn more about how wineries inter-act with various ministries of the Ontario government. Hillebrand was one of the wineries they visited.

Soon after their visit, LCBO chairman Jack Ackroyd, with members of his staff and employees of Ontario's Ministry of Consumer and Commercial Relations (MCCR), toured the winery and enjoyed a wine tasting. We greeted them with our good news. In a competition spon-sored by Canada's External Affairs Department and International Trade Canada, in which 25 Canadian wine companies had entries, Hillebrand had come out on top. The tasting competition was held to see which Canadian wines would be offered at official functions in Canada and at Canadian diplomatic missions abroad. Six Hillebrand wines had been accepted, the largest representation of any Canadian wine company.

As in 1988, the first time the competition was held, wine critic and consultant Andrew Sharp supervised the competition. The judges were made up of a panel of leading wine critics from across Canada. The Hillebrand wines selected were: Riesling Cuvée (1988), Late Harvest Vidal (1988), Collectors' Choice Chardonnay (1987), Chardonnay (1988), Maréchal Foch (1988) and Riesling Cuvée Sparkling Wine.

The selection was announced by the Honorable Shirley Martin, minister of state representing the Right Honorable Joe Clark and International Trade Minister John Crosbie. In making the announcement, Minister Martin said, "Our country is producing fine wines—wines that we can be proud to serve anywhere in the world. Canadian wineries have been attracting attention recently by winning many awards at international wine competitions."

The sales of the varietals, and in particular Chardonnay, were growing faster than we had ever expected. This was largely due to our winemakers, who were expanding their quality-driven programs, producing five distinct styles of Chardonnay and three styles of Riesling. They adhered to their belief that quality varietal wines are created in the vineyards, in the cellar and from the philosophy of the winemaker. Greg Berti had forecast in 1987 that by 1990 the growers would be able to meet Hillebrand's requirement for Chardonnay grapes, and he was right.

During 1990 Hillebrand Winery released five distinct styles of Chardonnays:

- Harvest Chardonnay, 1989

- Barrel-aged selected vineyard Chardonnay, 1989

- Huebel Vineyard barrel-fermented Chardonnay, 1989

- Buis Vineyard barrel-fermented Chardonnay, 1989

- Collectors' Choice Chardonnay, 1989

The three distinct Rieslings were:

- Harvest Riesling, 1989

- Riesling Classic Dry, selected vineyards, 1989

- Canadian Inspirations Riesling Dry, 1988

Canadian Inspirations Riesling Dry was one of the most interesting Hillebrand releases of the year. It was produced using the best grapes from some of the top vineyards in the Niagara Peninsula. The dry summer of 1988 brought Riesling grapes to perfect maturity. The juice was extracted from our drip tanks as free-run juice after skin contact. This combination of superior grapes, Hillebrand's cellars and the talent of our winemakers made for a wine that deserved the name Inspiration.

The winery presented the Canadian Inspirations Riesling in a long, green bottle with a most unusual label designed by Laurie Le France. Canadian Inspirations was a dry Riesling, straw yellow in color, more intense and aggressive than the Classic, more floral, with notes of citrus fruit and peach, and apricot with a touch of honey. It was quite crisp on the palate, with good fruit intensity and a fresh, clean finish.

In April 1990, Hillebrand introduced the new Collectors' Choice Chardonnay, 1988 vintage, and Cabernet Merlot, 1988 vintage. Both wines featured labels with replications of paintings by Group of Seven artist Frederick Varley. (By sheer serendipity, in 1957, Frederick Varley had resided next door to our house on Lowther Avenue in Toronto.)

Hillebrand's 1988 Collectors' Choice Chardonnay was produced with great care by our winemakers, who had applied all their combined experience to create this VQA wine. Once the wine was finished, Hillebrand's carefully planned oak-ageing program was implemented. To add complexity the wine was aged in predominantly Allier and Troncais barrels for six months. The 1988 Collectors' Choice Cabernet Merlot had also received the VQA designation. Wine lovers found it smooth-textured, medium-bodied and well-balanced, with a lingering clean finish.

As in previous years, Hillebrand won many international awards in 1990:

International Eastern Wine Competition (U.S.)

Maréchal Foch, 1988 ~ *Bronze Medal*
Cabernet Merlot, 1988 ~ *Bronze Medal*
Chardonnay, 1988 ~ *Quality Wine Award*

Intervin International Competition (U.S.)

Collectors' Choice Chardonnay, 1988 ~ *Gold Medal*
Eiswein, 1987 ~ *Gold Medal*
Canadian Inspirations Riesling, 1988 ~ *Bronze Medal*

21st International Wine and Spirit Competition (U.K.)

Riesling Classic Dry, 1988 ~ *Trophy & Gold Medal*
Barrel-Fermented Chardonnay, 1988 ~ *Gold Medal*
Gamay Blanc, 1988 ~ *Silver Medal*
Chardonnay, 1988 ~ *Silver Medal*
Eiswein, 1988 ~ *Silver Medal*
Riesling Cuvée Sparkling, 1988 ~ *Silver Medal*
Canadian Champagne ~ *Silver Medal*
Collectors' Choice Cabernet Merlot ~ *Bronze Medal*

Cuvée 1990 (Niagara Falls)

Trius Red—Glenlake Vineyards, 1989 ~
Consumers' Choice, Top Red

Great Canadian Barrel Tasting

Hillebrand Estates' 1989 Chardonnays ⌁
***Nekah Plate*, Best Chardonnays at Barrel Tasting**

International Food and Wine Competition
(Académie du Vin)

Harvest Riesling, 1988 ⌁ *Best Dry White*
Riesling Cuvée Sparkling, 1988 ⌁ *Best Canadian Sparkling*

One day at the end of May 1990, quite unexpectedly, John Swan came to see me at my office in Toronto. Since we had met at Hillebrand just a couple of days before, I was surprised to see him. I soon found out the reason for his visit. John had made a very difficult decision to return to England for family reasons and would have to resign from his position as president at Hillebrand. I knew how dedicated John was to Hillebrand and how very difficult this decision must have been for him. He promised to stay until a new president could be appointed.

It was not an easy task to find a qualified person to replace John Swan. During his presidency at Hillebrand, John and his team had formulated goals, projections and expansion programs, including the introduction of new viticultural and vinification techniques, to bring Hillebrand's wines to international standards. Under John's guidance, his team of professionals had obtained prime shelf position in liquor stores. By 1990, Hillebrand had opened more than 40 company-owned retail stores and acquired licenses for several more stores to be opened no later than 1991. John had also been a founding member of the committee that had established the Vintners Quality Alliance in Ontario. And John had been at the helm when, in 1988, Hillebrand was awarded the Business Certificate of Merit in Marketing by the federal government.

With John's departure we looked for a new president who would understand and promote Hillebrand's philosophy and concept; a person who would have good general knowledge of the wine business, but specifically someone who had extensive experience in retail store management. We also needed a president who would show leadership in the area of financial controls and who could cultivate good relationships within the wine industry. It was a lot to look for.

The wine and spirit industry had gone through many transformations during my 39-year involvement in it. As a result of all these changes, there were few people who had the ability to run both a modern winery and an extensive retail operation. After discussing the situation with Emil Underberg and Helmuth van Schellenbeck, we decided to approach George Sorensen.

I had known George for many years during his long career in various capacities while he was with the Newfoundland Liquor Corporation. He had been appointed by the Newfoundland government as the first non-political president of the Newfoundland Liquor Corporation. During his presidency he had made changes to modernize the corporation, including upgrading retail stores. George, however, had wanted to make the move into the wine and spirit industry, and had courageously left his secure and prestigious position in Newfoundland to join Watley's, a small wine and spirit agency located in Toronto.

In early 1982 I had hired George, on a part-time basis, to either find a suitable site for building a winery or to locate a small estate winery that could be acquired by Underberg Company. After Emil Underberg purchased Newark Winery, Peter Mielzynski Agencies appointed George as vice president of its operations in British Columbia and Alberta. He was with the agency for a few years until, for family reasons, he went back to Newfoundland. He took a position with Fishery Products International in the retail sector of the company. In 1990 the government imposed severe restrictions on the fishing industry. Therefore, our offer to George to become the president of Hillebrand Estates Winery was timely. On July 1, 1990, we announced the appointment of George Sorensen as the new president of Hillebrand Estates Winery. John Swan offered to stay for a while in order to introduce George to the wine industry and to help acquaint him with the winery and its team.

Prior to leaving, John put into action another example of Hillebrand's philosophy of matching wine with the arts. We celebrated Hillebrand's first Annual Vineyard Jazz Festival in July 1990. The purpose of the two-day jazz festival was to encourage young people to come to the winery to listen to music and taste and enjoy our wines. Jeannie and Jimmy Cheatern and the Sweet Baby Blues Band, the Jimmy McGriff–Hank Crawford Quartet, Arthur Prysock and the Red Prysock Quartet, some of the biggest names in jazz, entertained the crowd of over 2,000 people. There was plenty of food and refreshments available as Hillebrand staff served jazzburgers, jazzdogs, cheese trays and Hillebrand's award-winning wines. Throughout the day we conducted special winery tours for the guests. Hillebrand's first Annual Vineyard Jazz Festival was a well-attended gala event, much enjoyed by those who attended. It would become a popular annual event that attracted wine lovers from far and near.

There was another celebration that summer. The prestigious Toronto restaurant Nekah hosted the Great Canadian Chardonnay Competition. Of 34 Chardonnays entered in the competition, Hillebrand won the prized Nekah Plate for achieving top honors.

Rather than rest on our laurels, we encouraged the sharing of ideas with other wineries both domestically and abroad. Whenever possible, Hillebrand invited wine experts to visit and offer criticism. James Sichel of Bordeaux, Jean Chartron from the home of Chardonnay in Burgundy and Jean Caillou from Pommery Champagne were a few of the distinguished guests who added to the exchange of ideas.

The initial quest for quality wines had paid off in the number of VQA-designated wines in the Hillebrand stable. One such wine was Hillebrand Harvest Chardonnay. From its introduction in 1989 this wine had attracted a keen following. The right price point combined with the right style of fruit-driven Chardonnay offered consumers real value. The sales of Harvest Chardonnay soared from 3,000 cases in 1990 to over 8,000 cases in 1992. During the same period, the number of barrels we were using increased from 250 to 342—a 37 percent jump. This reflected Hillebrand's commitment to barrel-aged quality wines.

Nationally our wine sales were impressive. In LCBO stores Hillebrand sales surpassed 90,000 cases, while our own stores topped this figure at 150,000 cases. We also won many international awards, including a gold for our Eiswein at the prestigious International Wine and Spirits Competition in the United Kingdom. In fact, there were a number of awards for us in 1991:

International Eastern Wine Competition (U.S.)

Harvest Riesling, 1989 ～ *Silver Medal*
Eiswein, 1989 ～ *Silver Medal*
Riesling Classic, 1990 ～ *Bronze Medal*
Riesling Cuvée Sparkling, 1990 ～ *Bronze Medal*

Intervin International Competition (U.S.)

Eiswein, 1989 ～ *Gold Medal*
Chardonnay, 1989 ～ *Silver Medal*
Late Harvest Vidal, 1989 ～ *Silver Medal*

Collectors' Choice Chardonnay, 1989 ~ *Bronze Medal*
Harvest Chardonnay, 1989 ~ *Bronze Medal*
Barrel-Aged Chardonnay, 1989 ~ *Bronze Medal*
Buis Vineyard Chardonnay, 1989 ~ *Bronze Medal*

22nd International Wine and Spirit Competition (U.K.) 1991

Eiswein, 1989 ~ *Gold Medal*
Barrel-Aged Chardonnay, 1989 ~ *Silver Medal*
Riesling Classic, 1989 ~ *Silver Medal*
Harvest Riesling, 1989 ~ *Silver Medal*
Barrel-Fermented Chardonnay—Buis Vineyard, 1989 ~ *Bronze Medal*
Gamay Blanc, 1990 ~ *Bronze Medal*
Canadian Inspirations Riesling Dry, 1988 ~ *Bronze Medal*
Late Harvest Vidal, 1988 ~ *Bronze Medal*
Riesling Cuvée Sparkling, 1990 ~ *Bronze Medal*
Canadian Champagne ~ *Bronze Medal*

By 1992 Hillebrand was not only the winery with the most awards in Ontario but also could claim to be the largest producer of varietal wines in Canada! With each new vintage, Hillebrand was setting the standards for Ontario quality wines. Trius had already won praise from journalists in 1990. With the launch of the 1989 vintage in 1991, we had a tremendous response from the consumers at our own stores, where we had set up displays to promote the Trius series.

Due to limited quantities, Trius was sold only at LCBO speciality stores initially. However, as the Trius Red, 1990, launched in November 1992, was a huge success, we had to assign a certain number of cases for the members of our wine club. An endorsement from Ontario journalist Bill Munnelly's *Best Bottles* magazine column is worth noting: "The 1990 vintage Trius red is the best tasting local wine I've ever drunk. Don't miss it." Our proudest moment came for

Trius when the new label was lauded as the top corporate label by the *Applied Arts* publication.

In November 1991, our Mounier Sparkling wine was launched. Timed for pre-Christmas release, and just in time to capture the festive year-end spirit, the investment of significant capital and labor was put to the test. The extensive cellar and stock, which had begun in 1989, now yielded 100,000 bottles. As with Trius, Mounier had been conceived with a European spark. The know-how of the Austrian *méthode champenoise*, combined with the financial support of Emil Underberg, had yielded Mounier. Mounier came on stage as a premium sparkling wine with a unique Canadian identity. To my son Robert, the concept was clear: "Mounier Brut is the result of the Niagara Peninsula culture, the result of years of replanting, re-evaluating and re-establishing the pick of the region's grape growers."

Bill Munnelly noted at the time: "I think Mounier is a landmark in the development of local wine, a bold commitment and a good result. This is what is needed. I like the spirit of Hillebrand."

As a result of Hillebrand's consistent emphasis on winery tours, the Mounier cellar became a unique and much-anticipated stop. This was a chance to see the time-honored tradition of European wine-making, with riddling racks, disgorging and dosage, in its new home in Niagara. Representatives from other champagne houses came by to exchange ideas.

Shortly after George Sorensen succeeded John Swan as president, I came to realize that the intense activities of the past years had taken their toll. My doctor told me to slow down or I would have to pay the consequences.

When we purchased Newark Winery in 1982, the credibility of Ontario wines was in serious question. By taking themselves seriously, Ontario winemakers and wineries had begun to discover the positive results of lower yields and the utilization of the best strains of vinifera in the most suitable soils. I felt very fortunate to have been part of not only Hillebrand's growth but also the development of the entire Niagara region.

Now my health told me it was time to pass the torch to the next generation. In October 1992, I submitted my resignation as chairman of Hillebrand Estates Winery. I maintained, of course, an active interest as a director at Hillebrand and continued to consult on various aspects of market development that I had helped to nurture from the start.

When I stepped back from Hillebrand in 1992, my efforts focused on helping my son Peter, as he was taking on more and more responsibilities at Peter Mielzynski Agencies. My passion for Hillebrand wines had assured an abiding presence for their wines in LCBO stores. With 22 general listings and sales of over 90,000 cases a year, the presence of Hillebrand in LCBO stores was enviable.

In 1994 Emil Underberg decided to sell Hillebrand. For over 12 years his efforts had provided the technical and financial support that had allowed Hillebrand to become a prestigious Canadian winery. Now, because of the dissolution of the Soviet Union's hold on Eastern Europe, many opportunities arose for new ventures closer to home. I offered my services to help him find the right buyer. John Peller, of Andrés fame, became the new owner of Hillebrand. Of his acquisition of Hillebrand, he said, "It is like buying a Lamborghini car." His words were a testament to the image that we had all sought to achieve since the Newark days, a little more than 12 years earlier.

I had never anticipated in 1982 that within a relatively short time we would have created a premium winery, which collected international awards and produced wines that would be found in celebrated restaurants. Or that we would have developed an exclusive line of varietals in distinctive bottles, which consumers clamored to buy.

Today, the Trius line of varietals and vineyard-designated wines are distributed across Ontario. These wines quickly disappear from the shelves until the next heralded vintage. The Trius Red is always among the top red wines produced in Ontario. I heard a local journalist state recently that of all the reds submitted for tasting (1998 vintage), Hillebrand's Trius was the best.

As a salesman, I was very proud of being able to change people's minds about wine by working with their preferences. High-quality wines really speak for themselves! I like to think that at Hillebrand we helped to turn people's attention toward Ontario wines. There was a collective enthusiasm within Hillebrand, with Peter Mielzynski Agencies, in the stores, in the tour groups, and among our grape growers, and that's what made the difference. In order to change people's perceptions about Ontario wines, we first had to take ourselves seriously and work at making the best wines possible. And that is what we did from the very early years at Hillebrand.

The successes of Hillebrand remind me of my first thoughts when I came to Canada more than 50 years ago. The raw beauty and tremendous potential of this land and its people immediately impressed me. At Hillebrand Estates Winery we somehow managed to harness and fulfill this potential in a lasting—and delicious—way.

Appendix 1

Hillebrand's Back Label Program

*O*ur wines contained detailed information on the back labels to inform and educate customers about the content and quality of our products. With this information we believed an intelligent and informed purchase decision could be made. The labels contained the following winemaking information:

Grape Variety Most important in the production of a fine wine is the use of quality wine varieties. At Hillebrand, our table wines are made only from classic vinifera and French-hybrid grapes. Our varietal wines are produced 100 percent from the grape variety on the label.

Harvest Date The correct harvest date is critical, with superior quality being possible only when the grapes are picked at the peak of perfection—properly matured, with sugar and acid balance appropriate to the wine being produced. Carefully determined by our winemakers, this decision ultimately dictates the quality of the wine.

Brix at Harvest This indicates the natural sugar content of the grapes when harvested. Hillebrand carefully limits production levels to ensure natural sugar content in the grapes. Quality is improved because all the vitality of the soil and vines is channeled into fewer grapes, resulting in greater flavor. At Hillebrand, the credo has always been Quality Is Better Than Quantity.

Total Acidity This number indicates the total number of all acidic compounds in the wine. As an indicator of the wine's character, the higher the number, the higher the acidity. A wine with 6.5 and above generally tastes fresh and crisp. A wine below 6.5 generally tastes softer and more mellow.

Total SO$_2$ While sulphur is not present in the grapes, it is found in all wines, a natural result of fermentation. Because it was found to be beneficial in keeping the wine fresh, SO$_2$ has been added since before Roman times. Even then it was known that wines produced with controlled SO$_2$ levels are far superior to wines without it. Fine winemakers through the generations have refined the practice, and at Hillebrand, levels of SO$_2$ are meticulously maintained at less than 150 parts per million (ppm). This is well below government standards permitting levels as high as: 200 ppm for dry reds; 300 ppm for dry whites; 300 ppm for sweet whites.

pH at Bottling Technically denoting the concentration of hydrogen atoms in the wine, pH normally increases as the total acidity decreases. For the winemaker, pH is an essential variable; for the consumer, it is of interest because it reinforces the total acidity indicator. A high number (over 3.50) means that the wine's acidity is well buffered and the wines will be mellow.

Residual Sugar This indicates the level of sweetness of the wine at the time of bottling and parallels the LCBO coding system. For example, a residual sugar level of approximately 1.0 percent corresponds to sugar code (1) in the LCBO scale. The higher the number, the sweeter the wine. Wines of higher sweetness levels should have higher total acidity to avoid being cloying and out of balance.

APPENDIX 2

EXCERPTS FROM *INSIDE WINE*

*I*n 1989, the Hillebrand Estates Winery developed a quarterly newsletter called *Inside Wine* for its Vintage Club members. Members of the club automatically received this newsletter, which was designed to better educate wine aficionados about the production and appreciation of wine. Excerpts from *Inside Wine, Winter 1990*, and *Inside Wine, Harvest, 1992* are reprinted below to give you a sense of the information our newsletter contained. (Excerpts are reprinted exactly as they appear in *Inside Wine*.)

THE MAKING OF REDS, WHITES AND ROSES

Following the article on the "Anatomy of Hillebrand," this article details the winemaking of red, white and rose wines. Although somewhat "procedural," an understanding of winemaking/vinification provides a basis with which to understand and appreciate various types of wines. Further articles on fining, oak aging, etc., will be presented in upcoming issues of Inside Wine.

White Wine

Grapes to Juice:

The objective of this phase of the white winemaking process is to extract juice and flavour from the grapes *without* colour and tannins.

White wine can be made from red or white grapes. If red grapes are used, the skins will be separated from the juice during fermentation (thus the colour from the skins is not extracted).

Firstly, the grapes are removed of *all* stems, leaves and twigs by the destemmer.

The grapes are then directed to the drip tanks whereby the "free run" juice is extracted. The weight of the grapes upon themselves provides for this high quality juice, utilized in the making of our finest varietal wines.

The Europress or Bucher Press
The remaining grapes then proceed to the Europress or Bucher press.

The Europress was imported from Germany in 1984 at a cost of $120,000. This press and the Bucher are only used at harvest time—for six weeks of the year.

Unlike conventional steel-on-steel presses, bladder presses inflate with air and gently massage the grapes. Thus, bitter oils from the seeds and excessive tannins from the stems are not released into the juice.

The Presses are also computerized, allowing the exact pressure to be maintained for the type of grape being pressed. One tonne [metric ton] of pressed white wine grapes provides approximately 700 L of juice. After pressing, skins and pumice are not wasted, they are returned to the field as a natural fertilizer.

The first stage of fining (clarifying) involves either use of the centrifuge or settling tanks. At Hillebrand, the centrifuge is used whereby the machine spins rapidly to remove solids from the wines.

Fermentation:

The objective of fermenting white wines is to transform the sugar into alcohol.

The process involves inducing fermentation with the addition of selected yeasts. Yeast consumes the natural sugar and converts it into alcohol and CO_2. The temperature must be maintained at 18° to 20°C throughout the fermentation. This low temperature extends the fermentation period, thus retaining the crisp fruitiness of the grape variety.

The centrifuge may again be used to extract the remaining yeasts for wines which require a certain residual sugar level.

Clarification:

The objective of clarification is to eliminate all solids from the wine and create a wine which is chemically and biologically stable.

The Wine Chiller

Many white wines are cold stabilized to avoid allowing any natural tartrate salts to precipitate. The wine chiller chills the wine to the point of freezing. Tartrates crystallize and are filtered out of the wine before bottling.

Tartrates sometimes form at the bottom of the bottle or at the end of the cork. This tends to cause some agitation among consumers who assume the tartrates are "grit" or glass. These so-called "wine diamonds" are actually a mark of high quality wines. However, Hillebrand uses the wine chiller to remove any such confusion.

The Diatome Earth Filter
A very unique and interesting filtration process is the diatomaceous earth filter. This filter utilizes tiny fossilized shells which are crushed into powder form. A "cake-like" film of powder is formed around the screens inside the machine. The wine passes through this sieve which catches unwanted yeasts and bacteria.

Filtering is again conducted prior to bottling to maintain the wine's stability.

Aging:

White wines require much less aging than reds. White wine will age in the steel vats for about 2 to 6 months before bottling. Constant monitoring and careful analysis ensure that the wine will develop properly.

Chardonnay is unique in its fermentation process and aging. Malolactic fermentation (discussed later) and oak aging are required. Upcoming issues will discuss the details of oak aging and fermentation for Chardonnays.

Red Wine

Grapes to juice:

The objective of this phase of the red winemaking process is to extract juice and flavour *with* colour and tannins. Red wines are made from only red grapes.

Again, the process involves the destemmer. Here anywhere from 60% to 100% of the grapes are removed of their stems. Some stems usually remain to provide the wine with body and to enhance the aging potential of the wine.

Red wine grapes are then routed to the Vinimatic. Red wine's characteristic colour and tannin is extracted from the skins of the grapes (the properties of the skin permeate into the juice naturally). In the Vinimatic, the skins are left on the grapes from 4 days to 3 weeks, depending on the grape variety. The Vinimatic is occasionally used for white wines, if the machine is not being used for red winemaking.

Fermentation:

Unique to red winemaking, the first fermentation takes place while the skins remain on the grapes. The three objectives of red wine fermentation involve 1) the transformation of sugar into alcohol 2) the extraction of colour and tannins 3) second or malolactic fermentation.

Alcoholic fermentation is induced in the Vinimatic with the addition of selected yeasts. The Vinimatic slowly rotates and an internal coil, heated by water, maintains the fermentation.

Temperatures for red wine fermentation are 25° to 35°C, the higher temperatures essential for colour and tannin extraction.

The grapes are then transferred to one of the Presses. Here one tonne of grapes provides 750 L of juice, somewhat more than for white wine grapes.

Alcoholic fermentation continues in the fermentation tanks until malolactic fermentation begins. Malolactic fermentation essentially involves the conversion of malic acid (apple-like acid) into lactic acid (milk-like acid), softening the wine. Temperatures for malolactic fermentation are 18° to 20°C.

The centrifuge is then used as for white wines.

Clarification:

As for white wines.

Aging:

The objectives of aging red wines are threefold; to give the wine more complexity, to soften the tannins, and to harmonize the wine's constituents.

Stainless steel tanks are employed when tannins require softening and the wine requires balance. When the red wine also requires complexity, the wine is aged in barrels anywhere from 2 months to 2 years.

The oak itself can contribute special flavour characteristics to wines. However, it is primarily the slow oxidation process (as oak barrels are slightly porous), which creates unique flavours and complexity.

Finally, bottle aging, a much slower process than barrel or tank aging, is applied to wines which require extended aging.

Rose Wine

Rose wines are made using red grapes. There are two distinct methods for creating rose wines.

Rose via white wine vinification:

Very ripe grapes are processed through the destemmer and are immediately pressed to extract colour.

The remainder of the vinification proceeds as for white wines. This method, although simple and quick, tends to create lower quality roses with weak body.

Rose via red wine vinification:

Grapes are removed of their stems via the destemmer. Skins are left on the grapes as for red wine, but for only 12 to 24 hours.

When the desired colour is achieved, the free run juice is drained from the tank. Utilization of the centrifuge, alcoholic and malolactic fermentation are all conducted as for red wine. However, no barrel aging is applied.

Although this method (used for Hillebrand's Elizabeth Rose) requires more equipment and time, it does produce a quality rose with fine flavour, body and complexity.

—J. L. Groux
Winemaker

—Ben Huchin
Winemaker

—Robert Mielzynski
Winemaker & Vice President

A WINE CELLAR?

Would you like to start a wine cellar or expand on your existing efforts at storing wines for future drinking? In a series of articles, we'll explore start-up considerations and progress to increased sophistication in 'cellaring' wine.

Hopefully this will remove some of the mystery associated with wine storage and, at the same time, instill an idea of what cellaring is all about and why many people get hooked on the concept. Most times when we get involved in a discussion with someone about their wine collection, it will be '82 Bordeaux, Sauternes, etc.—often a daunting subject because of its size and complexity. It doesn't have to be that way.

Most information on wine is related to European producers and recently California as well. In the past ten years, however, there's been a tremendous growth in many other areas of the world. Canada has been part of this explosion, where we see a significant number of really excellent wines being produced. With modern communication and technology, improvements in grape growing and winemaking are much faster. We need not travel abroad to find collectable wine any more. Much of our Ontario production is now being made with more body and structure, which will develop increased complexity and enjoyment if allowed to rest quietly for a while before consumption.

There are several good reasons to store wine. The first and most obvious is convenience. It's nice to know that you have a variety of wines handy when a bottle is wanted. There is the advantage of picking a particular wine from your stock irrespective of the situation—whether it be drop-in friends or Sunday dinner with your family.

Another is economy. Wine is often less expensive by the case lot, as it is for the Vintage Club member. As well, wine is usually less expensive on release than a year or two later due to inflation, our governments increasing taxation, and the cost of storage.

Third, and often most important to a typical wine lover, keeping your own 'cellar' permits you to lay away quantities of certain wines that improve with age. Most wine goes out of circulation within a year after being released by the winery. By buying the wines 'young' and laying them away, you have the chance to enjoy them when they are at their peak of quality. Flavours in many wines improve with proper aging, and in future articles here, we'll try to unlock some of the mystery on how to know and understand whether a wine should be aged or not, and if so, for how long.

There is another accepted reason for cellaring which initially is difficult to appreciate. It is, simply, very satisfying to have a collection of things that are dear and important to you in your home, and to wander among them from time to time, either alone or in the company of friends who can share your appreciation of them. Anyone who prizes a library of books or phonograph records knows exactly the feeling.

The intriguing thing about a cellar, that I have found personally, is the 'reliability' I'll call it. When a particular occasion presents itself, Christmas, Birthday, or whatever, I can choose a wine that is appropriate and *I can count on*. With several bottles of a single wine in the cellar, I know (having already tried it) what style, quality, and enjoyment it promises and I won't be disappointed. This can often be done by buying a wine, trying it, and going back for more at the particular time, but invariably it's gone from the store. Having my own supply gives me the chance to guarantee good 'celebration' wine. It helps in planning for good times!

—Rob W. Ball

Rob Ball is the President of the Niagara-on-the-Lake Amateur Vintner's Club. Rob is also a member of the American Wine Society, the Australian Wine Society, the Niagara Wine Guild and the Amateur Winemakers of Ontario. Rob has maintained a cellar for six years, although his latest and most exciting cellar, he has had for three. This cellar, located below the basement level, is circular with a spiral staircase, is made of fibreglass and holds 511 bottles in clay tile wine racks. The inventory is maintained on Hugh Johnson's computer system for cellaring. Certainly an impressive tour for guests!

LIFE IS A CABERNET

Life is a Cabernet—a look at Cabernet Sauvignon around the World

Of all the noble black grape varieties planted in vineyards through-out the world, there can be little argument that the Cabernet Sauvignon reigns as the uncrowned king. This is not to suggest that any Cabernet-based wine will be superior to a Pinot Noir-based wine, a Merlot-based wine, a Nebbiolo-based wine, or any other red wine for that matter. What makes Cabernet Sauvignon so great is its ability to not only produce complex, intriguing, age-worthy wines, but its ability to yield such wines in almost any region in which it is planted. From its native ground in the fields of Bordeaux, France, to the AVAs (Approved Viticultural Areas) of California, the distant vineyards of Australia and South Africa, the hillsides of central Italy, Ontario's Niagara Peninsula, and scores of other diverse settings, the Cabernet Sauvignon consistently yields some of the world's most sought-after oenophilic masterpieces. And though many of these wines can be radically different in terms of style, the Cabernet Sauvignon's unmistakable character always manages to dictate their ultimate taste profile.

Part of the Cabernet Sauvignon's success lies in its ability to adapt, with little fuss, to a range of environmental conditions. The vine's small, dark, tough-skinned grapes are very hardy and resistant to disorders such as coulure (poor pollination due to bad weather resulting in sparse yields and often leading to millerandage—the failure of fruit to develop properly) and grey rot—a fungus which thrives in warm, damp conditions, attacking vine leaves and fruit and imparting unpleasant flavours. The Cabernet Sauvignon gives intensely coloured, tannic wine with a characteristic aroma of blackcurrant, often with some herbal overtones. Pure Cabernet Sauvignon wines tend to be on the harsh side. In order to balance the wine's power, other grape varieties, in particular the softer

Merlot, are often blended in with the Cabernet wine. Oak aging is also used extensively in Cabernet Sauvignon-based wines to soften the tannins and add complexity. Most Cabernet wines benefit from some degree of bottle aging.

France

The region of Bordeaux in western France, in particular, the Médoc—the wedge of land which stretches north from the town of Bordeaux to the Atlantic—is generally regarded as being Cab country par excellence. The special combination of riverside gravel banks and maritime climate helps the Cabernet vines bear concentrated fruit, rich in colour, tannin, and extract. The wines of the Médoc are never made strictly from Cabernet Sauvignon alone. Other varieties, including Merlot, Cabernet Franc, and Petit Verdot are used to round off the Cabernet Sauvignon's edges. The percentage of Cabernet Sauvignon used depends on each Château's particular style. The wine of Château Mouton-Rothschild in the Médoc commune of Pauillac, for example, could contain up to 85% Cabernet Sauvignon, while Château Rauzan-Gassies in the commune of Margaux may contain only 40% of this variety.

To truly understand the mysteries of a fine Cabernet-based Bordeaux you will need either a) patience or b) money. Bordeaux's great Cab-based wines need time to mature, ten years is often a minimum. Buying them young, when you might be able to afford them, and waiting for them to "come around" takes "a." Buying a fully mature Bordeaux, from a great year and of a great Château, takes a daunting amount of "b." Take your pick. A great, fully mature Bordeaux is often said to have a bouquet reminiscent of cigar box, blackcurrant, coffee, chocolate, plum, violets, and a veritable potpourri of spices, combined with a powerful yet ethereal flavour. Or so I've read.

California

The Cabernet Sauvignon has, over the past 30 years or so, established itself as the premier black grape variety of the country's North Coast, in particular, the Napa Valley. Due to the increased amount of sunshine and heat, the grapes tend to ripen earlier than in Bordeaux. Consequently, the resulting wines tend to be higher in alcohol, somewhat rounder, and approachable earlier than their French counterparts. Cabernets from the North Coast most closely resemble those of Bordeaux, a resemblance which begins to fade as you move further south and inland. Cabernets from the Central Coast, particularly Santa Barbara and Monterey, can often be overly herbaceous or vegetal in flavour.

In addition to the deep, dark, brooding style of the typical Californian Cabs, there is also a fair amount of Cabernet Sauvignon rosé produced. It's hard to imagine what a rosé made from such an intense grape variety is like, suffice to say that it's nothing like the red wines made from Cabernet Sauvignon. It is, however, very enjoyable, showing a very light ruby colour and smelling unmistakably of strawberries.

At present time there are approximately 30,000 acres in total of Cabernet Sauvignon planted in California. Napa leads in acres planted, followed by Sonoma, Monterey, San Luis Obispo, Lake County, and Mendocino.

Australia

The Cabernet Sauvignon has become an increasingly important grape variety in Australia. While the Shiraz (the Syrah of France's Northern Rhône Valley) still ranks number one on the list of popular grape varieties, Cabernet Sauvignon has ousted Grenache from second place and is fast encroaching on Shiraz's lead.

Australian Cabernets are steadily improving in quality, although, as with many other countries using Cabernet, it is often blended with other varieties (in this case with Shiraz) in order to obtain a better balanced wine. Coonawarra, a remote area approximately 236 miles southeast of Adelaide, has become the centre of Australia's Cabernet industry. The region's unique soil—a layer of terra rossa covering a bed of deep, porous limestone—and cooler than average climate have lead to the area being dubbed Australia's answer to the Médoc. Other areas which produce outstanding Cabernets are Victoria's Goulburn Valley and the Margaret River and Swan Valley areas of Western Australia.

Like California, Australia also produces Cabernet Sauvignon rosé, which is quite similar to the Californian model and extremely popular in its home country.

Spain

While not an authorized variety, Cabernet Sauvignon has been planted on an experimental basis in many of Spain's best wine producing areas with generally favourable results. The most recognized and celebrated Spanish Cabernet is undoubtedly the Coronas "Black Label," a 100 percent Cabernet Sauvignon wine produced from Bodegas Torres Mas La Plana vineyard in the Penedés region. Another Spanish Cabernet Sauvignon which has gained an international following is that of Jean León. Owned by a Los Angeles restaurateur, the Jean León winery produces some 20,000 bottles of Cabernet Sauvignon wine in a rich, intense, tannic style, often needing many years of bottle age before becoming approachable.

The ultra-modern Raimat estate near Lérida (now owned by the giant sparkling wine firm of Codorníu) has also succeeded in producing some excellent Cabernet-based wines, including "Abadia" and "Raimat Cabernet Sauvignon." In central Spain, Marqués de Griñon has been producing some excellent Bordeaux-style Cabernets, having had the advantage of working with the famous French wine guru Emile Peynaud and the late Alexis Lichine. The Marqués de Riscal winery in the demarcated area of Rueda in Old Castile has also been instrumental in the pioneering of Spanish Cabernet Sauvignon-based wines.

Italy

With the international success of such wines as Sassicia, Tignanello, Solia and other "Super Tuscans," Cabernet Sauvignon has become an increasingly important variety in Italy. While much of the Italian wine labelled "Cabernet" is usually northern Italian Cabernet Franc, bottled fresh and fruity without oak aging, Cabernet Sauvignon, aged in small French barriques, has sparked international interest. Angelo Gaja, a Piedmontese producer of bank-busting Barbarescos, has produced "Darmagi"—a Cabernet Sauvignon produced from relatively young vines planted on one of Barbaresco's best sites. It has already won many prizes and much praise, and is priced in the typically Gajaesque fashion.

The region of Breganze, one of a number of northern Italian Cabernet-producing DOCs, has been producing some of the country's most notable Cabernet Sauvignons. The single-vineyard "Palazzotto" and "Fratta" Cabernets from Maculan are two of Italy's best.

Perhaps Cabernet's most remarkable achievement in Italy is the impact it has had on the Tuscan wine industry. The Antinori family has always been associated with innovation and maverick winemaking. Ignoring traditional blending regulations, and in doing so opting out of a DOC classification, Marchese Piero Antinori began blending regional Sangiovese (the traditional Chianti grape) with Cabernet. So impressive were the results that a host of other Chianti producers followed suit, resulting in the creation of a new category of Italian wines known as Predicato. The term Predicato di Biturica applies to

Sangiovese/Cabernet blends, while Predicato di Cardisco applies to wines based predominantly on Cabernet Sauvignon.

Ontario

Ontario winemakers have jumped on the Cabernet bandwagon with typical enthusiasm and determination. And while Ontario Cabernets may appear as relatively recent additions to the province's varietal revolution, enthusiastic vineyard owners had planted Cabernet Sauvignon on an experimental basis as far back as 1973. It has been the vineyard owners that have accelerated the degree of quality to which Ontario Cabs have risen. Jean-Laurent Groux, Winemaker at Hillebrand Estates Winery comments: "Niagara has a very favourable climate for Cabernet Sauvignon, with more heat and sunshine than most of Europe's more northerly vineyards. This fact, combined with a shorter, but more intense growing season, gives us grapes of excellent concentration and balance. But we must not overlook the impact the individual growers have had. They've lowered yields, increased their knowledge and, in general, have really managed to get a handle on this variety."

With their Trius red wine, Hillebrand has constructed a Cabernet Sauvignon/Cabernet Franc/Merlot blend based on the Bordeaux model, with an emphasis on balance, finesse, and elegance rather than sheer power. Response from international wine experts has been extremely positive.

Life is a Cabernet . . .

The success of Cabernet Sauvignon is by no means limited to the areas we've explored. Pretty well every country in the world that makes wine is either using it extensively or continually experimenting.

South America, South Africa and Eastern Europe all have extensive plantings of this variety. Areas of France outside of Bordeaux are using Cabernet, either on its own or in blends with local varieties. And there can be little doubt that countries already using Cabernet Sauvignon will create better, more interesting, and more varied wines as vinicultural and viticultural practices continue to improve.

—Tod Stewart
Tod Stewart is a Toronto-based wine writer, consultant and educator.

WHAT IS "ASSEMBLAGE"?

The shortest definition could be: a blending process of different wines in judiciously chosen proportions to achieve a better wine than each of the individual wines on their own. But it is much more. . . .

Many techniques used in oenology (winemaking) require observations, knowledge, and experience of the winemaker. One, more than others, is "assemblage."

The quality of a vineyard and the climatic characteristics of a vintage make a wine more or less rich in aromatic compounds, structural compounds, colour compounds, etc . . . Winemakers endeavour to get the best out of the grapes with which they ferment. Wine then, is the result of a complex equation between the natural side (vineyard, climate . . .) and action from man.

Assemblage originated a few centuries ago in European vineyards where, for obvious economic reasons, vineyards with only one grape variety were expanded to include 3, 4 or 5 varieties until, the most extreme, 13 different varieties evolved in Chateauneuf du Pape region in France.

Harvested at the same time, these varieties were mixed in one fermentation tank. The wine quality produced was always average and not very different from year to year.

Understanding that there were advantages to taking the best aspect from each grape variety, wine producers realized that they could enhance the general quality of a blended wine by exploiting the best virtues of each variety.

An important improvement was to separately vinify all of the grape varieties in anticipation of the final blend.

Over the years wine producers learned, by managing this technique, to perfect their wines using the right proportions of each component, thereby creating a unique identity for a wine made in one area. (Witness Chianti, Rioja, Liebfraumilch, etc.)

Today, the most well-known "assemblage" is used for the making of *méthode champenoise* sparkling wines. After the fermentation, wines from different varieties, different vineyards, and different vintages are tasted and blended to make a "Cuvée." The Cuvée is the secret blend of each *méthode champenoise* producer.

At Hillebrand, the "assemblage" is not only the basis of the Cuvée for our *méthode champenoise* MOUNIER, but also of our TRIUS Red. More than a simple technique, "assemblage" summarizes the philosophy of our Trius.

To select the best vineyards of Cabernet Franc, Cabernet Sauvignon and Merlot, to adapt updated tools and equipment to our needs, and to focus during the whole winemaking process towards quality, is only worthwhile if there is proper assemblage.

Finishing with an entire day of tasting to make the final blend, a premium wine is born every year the second May after the vintage (i.e., 18 months after harvest), Trius Red, however, exists in the vineyard before harvest in the winemaker's imagination.

The winemaker must balance the aromas, the flavours, the feel of the wine on the palate, the tannins, the acidity, the colour, and the oak. All this brings many wines together to create one wine which is superior to all.

This art of assemblage takes time. It is complex, exciting, and the result is simple and fantastic.

Numerous wine shows, awards, prizes and trophies accredited to Trius Red 1989 and 1990 are important as they show that others appreciate our art—assemblage.

—Laurent Dal'Zovo
Winemaker

Glossary

Appellation:	Designated viticultural (grape-growing) areas of origin (e.g., Niagara Peninsula, Pelee Island, Lake Erie North).
Bidule:	In *méthode champenoise* production, the yeast mixture in the neck of the bottle.
Brix:	Measurement of natural sugar contained in grapes. A minimum count of brix allowed in different grape varieties is needed prior to the production of wines.
Brut:	Relates to champagne's dryness.
Cold stabilization:	The chemical process that ensures that the wine will be clear.
Cuvée:	A blend of wines to produce a particular style of finished wine.
Demi-sec wine:	Semi-dry wine.

De-stemming: The process of removing the stems from the grapes.

Disgorging: The process of removing yeast from the bottles.

Estate bottled: An estate bottled wine is one made entirely from grapes grown on land controlled by the winery.

Estate winery: A winery that produces and bottles its own wine on its own property.

Free-run juice: The juice that results when the weight of the grapes act as a press.

Grape-must: Newly pressed juices of grapes ready for fermentation.

Hoch: German wines from the Rhine region of Hochheim. In English, this word is often spelled "hock."

Hybrid grape: Grapes produced from different vine varieties between North America and vinifera from Europe that have been genetically crossed to produce grapes and required (European style) taste (e.g., Maréchal Foch, Seyval Blanc).

Labrusca grape: North American indigenous grape variety with an unpleasant "foxy" character.

Liqueur de tirage: Sugar dissolved in wine to help the second fermentation.

Liqueur d'expédition: Sugar dissolved in wine to help sweeten the final product.

Méthode champenoise: The classic (and most costly) method of producing sparkling wine; it involves bottle fermentation.

Méthode Charmat: A method for producing sparkling wine that involves tank fermentation; much less expensive than *Méthode champenoise*.

Méthode cuvée close: *See* Méthode Charmat.

Micro-climate: Local geographic area (e.g., by the lake, on the Niagara Escarpment) that provides different growing conditions through the interaction of the weather and the soil.

Oenology: The study and production of wines.

Poignettage: Shaking the bottles to loosen up yeast particles.

Press house: The building that houses the equipment for grape crushing; the heart of the winery.

Riddling: To move the deposit of yeasts and adjuvants into the bidule in the neck of the bottle.

Still wines: Every wine that is not sparkling or crackling; most wines fall into this category.

Tannin: Astringent substance caused by crushing grapes harshly.

Tartrates: Compound, mainly potassium hydrogen, found in many fruits; colorless crystalline, present in grape juice and deposited during the fermentation of wines.

Terroir: The wine-growing environment, covering soil, site and local climate.

Varietal wine: A wine made from 100 percent of a specific grape and stated in the label as such.

Viniculture:	The knowledge and process of producing wine.
Vinifera:	European vine stocks (e.g., Chardonnay, Riesling, Cabernet Sauvignon).
Vinified:	The production of wine (the process of making wine).
Vintage:	Year of harvest of grapes in producing wine.
Viticulture:	The knowledge and science of cultivating grapevines.

INDEX